Essentially
IRISH

Essentially IRISH

HOMES WITH CLASSIC IRISH STYLE

JOSEPHINE RYAN

PHOTOGRAPHY BY JAMES FENNELL

RYLAND
PETERS
& SMALL

LONDON NEW YORK

for Tomhaggard

DESIGNERS
Paul Tilby and Barbara Zuñiga

COMMISSIONING EDITOR
Annabel Morgan

LOCATION RESEARCH
Josephine Ryan and Jess Walton

CONTRIBUTING EDITOR
Helen Ridge

PRODUCTION
Gordana Simakovic

ART DIRECTOR
Leslie Harrington

PUBLISHING DIRECTOR
Alison Starling

First published in 2011 by
Ryland Peters and Small
20–21 Jockey's Fields
London WC1R 4BW
and
519 Broadway, 5th Floor
New York, NY 10012

www.rylandpeters.com

10 9 8 7 6 5 4 3 2 1

Text © Josephine Ryan 2011
Design and photographs
© Ryland Peters & Small 2011

ISBN: 978-1-84975-158-2

Library of Congress cataloging-in-publication data
Ryan, Josephine.
  Essentially Irish : homes with classic Irish style /
Josephine Ryan ; with photography by James Fennell.
-- 1st ed.
     p. cm.
  Includes index.
  ISBN 978-1-84975-158-2
  1. Interior decoration--Ireland--Themes, motives.
I. Fennell, James. II. Title. III. Title: Homes with
classic Irish style.
  NK2046.A1R93 2011
  747--dc23
                        2011023584
A CIP record for this book is
available from the British Library.

Printed and bound in China

INTRODUCTION

My father spent 30 years of his life in England, '~~a foreign land~~'. Like so many
of Ireland's sons and daughters, he left to find work and took a one-way ticket
from Dun Laoghaire to Holyhead in 1950. He met and married my mother,
a Jersey girl, and they made a home and a family; an English family of one girl
and one boy. Having come from a family of 13, my father would have liked
a bigger brood, but my mother was having none of it.

My father's yearning to come home was a constant. In June 1974, he realized
his dream and we left suburban St Albans in a white Triumph Toledo, with
Dandy the Jack Russell and Beauty the cat, to make the final return journey on
that ferry. We rented a dilapidated 1950s cottage in Herbertstown, County
Limerick. It was a summer I'll never forget because this time it was not a
holiday. We were not going back. We did the rounds of the aunts and uncles,
and my brother Paul and I hung out with our numerous cousins. September
came and I joined the De la Salle Convent in a town called Hospital before
changing to St Mary's Convent of Mercy in Newport, County Tipperary.
There, as hard as I tried to change my accent, I was always the English girl!

The other pursuit of that heady summer was the question of where to live.
We looked at many properties, but the only one that I can remember, as clearly
as if it were yesterday, was a fine Georgian farmer's house at the crossroads of
Caherline. I was desperate for my father to buy that house, with its sweeping
drive and fanlight above the front door. Alas, it was not to be. The farmer
decided not to sell and instead my father bought a piece of land in County
Limerick and built a bungalow. But the want of such a house has never left
me and, maybe, one day I will find my own Georgian house at a crossroads,
for as Mike Scott of the Waterboys sang, 'Ireland is my heart'.

Prior to the Great Famine, the population of Ireland reached in excess of
eight million. The majority of the people built simple 'houses', often referred
to as cottages, even though that was an English term, and when one thinks of
Ireland today, images of whitewashed thatched dwellings spring to mind.

In medieval Ireland, the High Kings built vast castles and towers. Many
now are ruins, but as many again are still inhabited. For much of its existence,

Dublin was a medieval city, but now it is famous for its Georgian architecture, which was first established on the north side of the city. Georgian houses, singly often referred to as the 'big house', were also built across the country. Many were destroyed during the Troubles of 1919–23, while others were neglected and fell into decay. Today, many are still standing. Some are maintained as homes by old families; others are cared for by the government or run as hotels.

Loved by millions, loathed by many, the bungalows of the 1950s and '60s have changed the face of the Irish landscape forever. With the arrival of the Celtic Tiger in the 1990s, there followed a building epidemic, when estates of identical houses were constructed across the country. Twenty-first-century

Ireland is a multicultural society, but it still has a firm grip on its culture and is proud of its history, albeit turbulent. Many of its emigrants have returned home, bringing lifestyles and influences learned in foreign lands.

All these factors, combined with the country's architectural history, make it hard to define exactly what is Irish style, and the houses featured in this book, which are all very different, bear witness to that. Maybe it's down to the weather and the extraordinary light, or to a secret ingredient akin to what makes the distinct taste of Guinness! Or it could simply be the uniqueness of the Irish spirit. Sigmund Freud got it right, I think, when he said of the Irish, 'This is one race of people for whom psychoanalysis is of no use whatsoever.'!

Simple
IRISH

Both Kim and Susan Dreyer were brought up not far from the sea — he in Denmark, she in Ireland — and they also met by the sea, on the Greek island of Symi. But this was destined to be more than a holiday romance.

GREAT DANE

Even though Kim returned to Copenhagen, to his architectural practice, and Susan to London and the busy, high-powered world of advertising, after a period of long-distance courting, Kim followed his heart and moved to the big city to be with Susan. London was their home for 15 years but, after the birth of their second child, Susan, not wanting to grow old in a city or in a foreign land, instigated their move to the 'auld country' and to be near the sea once more.

The couple decided to build a home from scratch, so bought just under an acre of land in beautiful County Wicklow, with its rolling soft hills, woodland, mountains and sea, on the east coast of Ireland. Conveniently situated just 29 miles south of Dublin via one of

ABOVE *Although olive trees are not usually associated with Ireland, they are, surprisingly, often hardy enough to survive the harsh winters. This mature specimen is the main feature in the middle of a paved terrace.* **RIGHT** *There are no obvious room delineations in the heart of this newly built eco-house. The expansive living and dining room areas merge seamlessly into one other and, in turn, into the kitchen.*

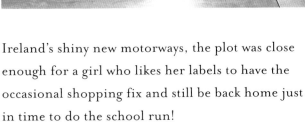

Ireland's shiny new motorways, the plot was close enough for a girl who likes her labels to have the occasional shopping fix and still be back home just in time to do the school run!

During the time it took for their joint vision to be realized, the couple rented a property locally and finally moved into their new home during the summer of 2006. Tucked down one of Wicklow's

CLOCKWISE FROM ABOVE *This tall, narrow window and piles of seasoned logs are artistically styled, creating a dramatic still life; An arrangement of dried foliage reflects the tones in the painting by Susan displayed behind; Simple, unadorned flatware and Waterford Crystal carafes are the obvious choices for relaxed dining; A single, oversized metal pendant lamp hanging low over the dining table provides the ideal lighting for intimate suppers.*

winding lanes, their timber-clad house has a distinctly Scandinavian feel. With geo-thermal heating, insulated with Irish sheep's wool and decorated with chemical-free eco paints manufactured in the neighbouring county, the house's carbon footprint is minimal. The roof slates are reclaimed, and a pair of 200-metre-deep wells on the land provide pure, soft and free water.

Sustainable this house may be but – thank goodness – its owners are not so committed as to rule out the primeval pleasures of open fires. A modest entrance hall belies what is to follow. The cast-stone staircase is pure sculpture. Not immediately visible, it leads to no less than seven levels. Beyond this lies the body of the house, an enormous, lofty space incorporating the kitchen,

ABOVE *A huge island is the main focus of the kitchen and provides a multifunctional work space. Inexpensive and easily manipulated, concrete has been used to create this bespoke installation, which includes recesses for cookery books, stools, a wine rack and storage baskets. The side facing the oven has large drawers for storing essential but less attractive cooking gadgets and kitchen paraphernalia. Topped with a thick piece of white-oiled French oak, the island also incorporates a small sink.*

dining and living areas, all linked by wide, salvaged floorboards of French oak. The soaring, dramatic ceiling trusses are constructed from green oak felled on a neighbour's farm. In this downstairs space, there are four different styles and sizes of window, all in total harmony with each other and each offering a different vista, and three sets of

double doors that open out onto a paved terrace, which becomes an outside room in summer.

Kim's original career path was to be a furniture designer – his ideal commission would be to design a house and everything that goes in it. Unsurprisingly, he has designed much of the furniture in his own home, including the elegantly minimal flamed beech dining table, which he had made locally. Classic Eames DSR chairs complement it perfectly.

OPPOSITE *Designed by Kim, the staircase is a combination of white monolithic forms. It was conceived as a three-dimensional sculpture, with a dual purpose — as a staircase and as an object to observe in the glazed space. It is separated from all adjacent surfaces so that it appears to float.*

ABOVE *The large sunroom, painted in Farrow & Ball's Hay, has the only walls in the house bearing a distinct colour. The array of cushions in the same tones and a cotton rug used as a tablecloth all give a feeling of warmth, even on the dullest of days.*

LEFT *In a vignette glimpsed from the hall, a pair of antique hay forks are put into service as hatstands!*

The kitchen units, made of plastered and painted concrete blocks, have a Mediterranean feel. To the right of the main fireplace is what looks like a simple trunk, but it is, in fact, an unusual piece of furniture from Vietnam, originally intended for storing food. Above this is the only artwork in the room, a beautiful textural abstract painted by Susan. She does, though, have ambitious plans for a huge canvas to fill the 'difficult wall' behind the hanging Egg chair, originally designed in 1959 by Danish designers

Nanna and Jørgen Ditzel, and now considered a classic. It typifies the naturalist theme seen in much Scandinavian design but, most importantly, it's amazingly comfortable to sit in, too!

The corridor to the left of the entrance hall leads to the children's bedrooms and the sunroom, not something you would generally expect to find in an Irish home. However, this large and comfortable room, reminiscent of an Italian loggia, with two huge glass windows on swinging pivots, has the right aspect, so even on the greyest

ABOVE LEFT *The family room is home to two cosy Ikea sofas covered in natural linen and draped with fragments of kilims and a tempting variety of tactile throws and blankets.*

TOP RIGHT *Extra blankets of silk, cashmere, wool and plaid are stacked on the low, kilim-covered coffee table.*

ABOVE RIGHT *A neat, small trunk makes a useful side table as well as offering concealed storage space for magazines.*

RIGHT *A large kilim, hung on the family room wall like a painting, fits the space like a glove. The loose arrangement of rust-coloured dried bracken falling over the antique trunk, with its wonderful patina of age, echoes the natural hues in the room.*

of days it is an energizing place to be. On sunny days, it is heavenly.

The subtle palette of whites, greys and taupe continues throughout the house, and not just in the wall paints either – the soft furnishings, upholstery and furniture follow the same theme. Susan is more comfortable with 'non-colour', making an exception only in her choice of kilims, which have been dyed with natural pigments and are used as paintings and a table covering in the more intimate family television room. She also

prefers large vases of greenery to flowers. Conveniently, their neighbour grows eucalyptus for the Dublin flower trade, so Susan buys a bunch from him every week, loving it for its sculptural form and aromatic fragrance.

The upstairs reading room and master bedroom follow the same design aesthetic of simplicity and purity. Kim designed the bed himself, yet it is perfectly compatible with the very traditional 19th-century veneered chest of drawers that sits alongside. The en-suite bathroom is a combination of ultra-modern Vola fittings and a vintage bathtub, with the original taps/faucets. A large picture of pears above the bath is an enlarged, grainy photograph taken by a friend,

OPPOSITE ABOVE LEFT *The ornate mirror with candle sconces is an unexpected addition to the modern basin in the small guest bathroom.*

OPPOSITE BELOW LEFT *Six French enamelled metal tiles create an arresting artwork on the hall wall.*

OPPOSITE ABOVE RIGHT *A large acrylic painting by Susan has pride of place at the end of the hall.*

ABOVE *The uncluttered main bathroom has concealed storage to the right of the sink unit. Above the bathtub hangs a picture of pears, photographed by a friend.*

LEFT *The main entrance belies what lies beyond. The hallway is relatively conventional, with French brushed limestone flooring, a painted sideboard from Indonesia and a large, ornate painted French mirror leaning against the far wall.*

BELOW *A lofty, attic-like space overlooks the dining and living area, making a comfortable and snug den. A pair of director's chairs sit within easy reach of a massive pile of delicately balanced paperbacks, while the fitted shelving beneath the dormer window runs all the way around the room and provides a display surface as well as offering additional seating with comfortable cushions.*

Carol Booth, who also made and gilded the large mirror – a surprisingly ornate addition to this simple interior.

Sandwiched between the master bedroom and the main bathroom is a modest, open-plan his-and-hers dressing room. A discreet peep at the carefully colour-coded rails of Kim's white cotton shirts and Susan's taupe cashmere jumpers reveals that the elegant 'non-colour' palette of the interior decoration is emulated in their wardrobe. It's a good job that sheep don't have blue wool – that would cause a huge dilemma chez Dreyer!

RIGHT *John Hinde 1950s postcards of Irish towns and countryside are classics.*
FAR RIGHT *Kim's Panama hats and Susan's jewellery on the chest of drawers follow the same colour scheme as the rest of the house.*
BELOW *In the bedroom, a kilim on the wall and a painting by Danish artist Hans Andersen propped up on the chest of drawers are the extent of the room's adornment.*

LEFT *Dingle Horse Riding caters to those tourists visiting the Dingle Peninsula who want to see the area on horseback, rather than by car, bus or bicycle.*

At the tip of the Dingle Peninsula, the fishing town of Dingle in County Kerry is the largest town in the Gaelic-speaking parts of Ireland, known as the Gaeltacht.

THE GREAT INDOORS

Built on a hill, Dingle or *Daingean Uí Chúis*, to use its Gaelic name, has a quite unique atmosphere: sophisticated and cosmopolitan with a hippy edge. Dingle came to the attention of the outside world in 1970 with the release of *Ryan's Daughter*, which was filmed there. Photos of its leading man Robert Mitchum are still to be seen on pub walls, and DVDs of the film are for sale everywhere. Then, in 1983, a dolphin took up residence in Dingle Bay and lives there to this day. He has become a huge attraction, and for some people swimming with Fungi is one of life's most magical experiences.

The town is still steeped in tradition and has more than its fair share of pubs, most of them hosting live music – it is estimated there is one bar for every ten men, and the population is approximately 1,200! There is also a choice of fine

The kitchen is a marvellous mix of furnishings. Seating is provided by a traditional Irish Súgán chair, alongside a Parisian-style bistro table, and a captain's chair at the gate-leg, drop-leaf pine table. A little pine bureau supports a contemporary Irish painting.

ABOVE *Súgán is Gaelic for 'straw' or 'straw rope', and this material was used to make chair seating throughout the Celtic world. These areas produced some unique and distinctive styles of furniture, such as this sugan chair with its original red paint.*

seafood restaurants, craft shops selling work by local artisans and more art galleries than you could shake a stick at. The very best of these is the Greenlane Gallery, owned and run by Susan Callery. Her other branch is in Paris! She travels there frequently, but it's a much closer commute to the Dingle gallery, just a five-minute drive from her home, which is filled with the work of the artists she represents.

Daughter of Dingle's illustrious solicitor Peter Callery (recently deceased) and a beautiful English mother, Susan was born and raised in a detached,

double-fronted Georgian property on Green Street (originally the Munster and Leinster Bank). However, she had no desire to live in another old house, so decided to have a house built to suit her and her family's requirements and to house her art collection. Susan also runs a riding school, meaning stables were needed for her 20 horses.

Susan's house was built just outside Dingle in 1998. From a distance, the bungalow, which is on an elevated site, looks no different from other such housing built around the same time. The driveway is lined in pillar-box red fencing with a life-sized wire sculpture of an Alsatian dog at the entrance, giving a hint of what's to come. The façade of the house is partially clad in old local stone, which would have been used for 18th-century cabins. The rest is whitewashed, with the hardwood windows left unpainted. It's the different roof levels that indicate that this house might not be as straightforward as you imagine.

The entrance is at the back, through the kitchen: a single-height space that opens into a soaring, double-height living room. This, in turn, becomes a vast dining room with unpainted stone walls and wood-panelled ceilings. A cathedral-sized window looks out to the stables and the sea.

Everything here is on a larger-than-life scale, befitting Susan's huge personality and boundless energy. In the kitchen, a bright red Aga is at the heart of the space, with an informal seating area comprising a pine captain's chair, a traditional red-painted sugan chair (*súgán* translates as rope made of hay or straw) and an old stripped-pine Irish drop-leaf circular table in front. The practical tiled floor at the cooking end of the kitchen gives way to pine flooring elsewhere.

ABOVE LEFT *The Dingle Races have taken place for almost 100 years, and every August they draw horses, jockeys and enthusiasts from all over Ireland and the rest of the world.*

ABOVE RIGHT *This bronze figure of a bull was one of the first pieces of Irish art that Susan bought when she was young.*

Offset beautifully by the flooring is an enormous 19th-century Irish dresser, with a built-in chicken coop. It's recently been painted white, which disguises its years. At the other end of the kitchen, a small-scale wood-burning stove is a source of extra warmth as well as an intimate place to sit and read. It's also where damp riding hats are often hung up to dry.

In the next two rooms, the scale is notched up a hundredfold. Three squashy, oversized modern leather sofas sit at right angles to each other in the living room, in front of a grand fireplace that's home to another wood-burning stove. The wooden Arts and Crafts-style mirror above the mantelpiece leans forward in trepidation, as do the sheep on the hillside behind the house. Standing on the hearth beside the spiral staircase, which leads to a mezzanine floor used for storage, is a large bronze stag, by Anthony Scott.

ABOVE *A wood-burning stove is far more efficient than an open fire, and this small model has the addition of a copper panel behind it to reflect heat back into the room. The wall of simple white tiles gives the fireplace a Scandinavian feel. Collections of natural objects found on country walks and rides — large pebbles, a piece of driftwood and a pair of antlers unearthed from a bog in County Roscommon — decorate the shelf above.*

RIGHT *In the dining room against a stone wall stands an unusual piece of early Chinese furniture. Placed artfully upon it are three very different pieces: a bronze contemporary female form, a 19th-century French carafe and a painted concrete base for a weather vane. The painting above by Irish artist Pauline Bewick is entitled* Lovers in Tuscany.

OPPOSITE ABOVE *The front part of the sitting room is also Susan's office. A leather-topped partner's desk, bought at auction, is married with an Eames chair that belonged to Susan's father. Sitting on the desk is a magnificent bronze sculpture of St Brendan's Voyage by Hans Blank.*

OPPOSITE BELOW *The generous fireplace offers a backdrop to Anthony Scott's sculptures of a majestic bronze stag, two vibrant blue horses and a noble Great Dane.*

The third wood-burning stove is situated in the dining room, occupying an imposing, white-painted modern fireplace with a bronze sculpture of a pod of whales by Hans Blank, a Dutch artist living locally. Two indoor plants, a *Monstera deliciosa* (cheeseplant) and a *Ricinus communis* (castor oil plant), have grown to jungle-like proportions in this light-filled space, cascading down from a shelf above the fireplace. The flooring in front of the hearth is Liscannor stone, a unique stone found near the cliffs of Moher in County Clare. It is instantly recognizable, as it displays dense fossilized imprints of marine activity. To the right and partially obscured by the cheeseplant, there is a built-in bookcase filled with catalogues from past gallery exhibitions and auction sale room guides.

Around the long French oak table are eight large, mismatched chairs and a wooden bench for four, providing the seating in a room that has seen many, many 'monstrously delicious' (pardon the pun!) and hilarious dinner parties. Standing with his back to the soaring windows and holding his arms out wide, as if to wish everyone *bon appétit*,

ABOVE *In the mistress's bedroom, the large, modern pine bed has been lime-washed, as has the carved Chinese trunk, a gift from Susan's mother, which is used as a bedside table. A random assortment of favourite Irish art adorns the pure white walls, all of it united by a vibrant jade-green hue that's echoed in the small statuette which stands on the decorative trunk beside the bed.*

is another bronze sculpture. This devilish creature is by one of Susan's favourite artists, Fidelma Massey. Susan sometimes puts a pair of candles in the palms of his hands.

The bedrooms at the opposite end of the house have equally high ceilings. The main bedroom has one wall that is all window. From Susan's lime-washed wooden bed, draped in a white cowhide and sitting on a pink and green Indian hand-woven silk rug, the only thing interrupting her view of the bay is a plinth in the middle of the garden, supporting a bronze cast by Bob Quin of a pair of laughing nuns doing a jig. White walls offer the perfect backdrop for the paintings, which are frequently exchanged, as elsewhere in the house, for others from the gallery.

The spacious, light-drenched bathroom has double glazed doors between it and the bedroom,

ABOVE LEFT *Sitting on a little pine stool beside the bathtub, the perfect form of this raku pot is purely decorative.*
ABOVE RIGHT *The bright and breezy en-suite bathroom is flooded with light, thanks to large skylights in the roof. The room successfully combines old and new elements, such as the oak Arts and Crafts overmantel hanging above the bath and the modern, chrome ladder towel rail, providing style as well as function.*

while another pair of large glass doors opens out onto the garden. The large, neutral-hued stone tiles used as flooring are repeated on the walls surrounding the panelled bath.

There are some pieces in her home that Susan admits she could never part with. One of them is the laughing bronze nuns. These lucky ladies will dance away their days in the magical kingdom of Kerry, which is exactly where Susan wants to be more than anywhere else in the world.

This converted barn, a mere 22 miles outside the city of Cork on the banks of the lovely River Lee, is in deep, lost countryside.

ASINUS DOMESTICUS

Ireland's new road network has drastically reduced driving times across the land but, once you turn off the 'N' roads, you find yourself on slow-moving country roads. These, in turn, become narrow, grassy boreens (lanes) and must be taken at a gentle pace. Just such a boreen, beyond Midleton in East Cork, leads to this isolated barn, as well as a Victorian farmhouse, both of which would fall into the sea if they were any nearer to the cliff edge. Being so close to Cork allows its

ABOVE *Chickens roam freely on the land at the side of the barn and provide more eggs than can be consumed. The different shades of shell are down to the different breeds.*

LEFT *The traditional kitchen is a delightful place to sit and decide how best you like your eggs! The red and white tea cosy on the countertop represents Cork's sporting colours.*

The 'press' in the kitchen is a
19th-century Irish piece of
furniture. A blackthorn stick
and a tattered donkey's lead
hang at the ready by the door.
The cudgel or cane, which
is known by many names,
has come to symbolize Irish
culture almost as much as the
shamrock. The saying goes: 'A
man without a blackthorn stick
is a man without an expedient'.

owner the enviable mix of a country and a city life without having to spend too much time in a car or on public transport.

Having renovated more houses than he cares to remember, the owner is always thinking about his next project. He came across his present home when out walking along the stunning coastline with some friends one weekend. Having always fancied a place along a boreen, he managed, 'between the jigs and the reels' (a fantastic Irish expression meaning comings and goings) to acquire the property, as well as a large chunk of land to go with it.

For most people, the abandoned Victorian farmhouse and barn would have proved too daunting a prospect for renovation. The house

ABOVE LEFT *The top half of the press is glazed, lending itself as a display cabinet for an eclectic and worldly collection of ware.*
ABOVE RIGHT *On the top shelf is a traditional china tea set of the sort you would expect to find at your grandmother's, alongside various utilitarian pudding bowls. These gain a wonderful patina as they age, provided they are not subjected to the cruelty of a dishwasher. On the middle shelf, either side of an Irish piece, are ornately glazed Moroccan terracotta bowls. Several pieces of original Irish spongeware are displayed at the bottom.*

had been empty for 50 years and was in a dire state of repair, with little but the outer shell salvageable. However, the owner was unfazed. With his astute vision and a reliable team of builders, the building was restored over a period of five years. It is now a comfortable hideaway where he loves to be.

ABOVE LEFT *Donkeys can live to a great age, and this carved wooden model has seen a fair few Christmases, as it would originally have been part of a Nativity set.*

ABOVE RIGHT *Political cartoons, such as this framed, Victorian hand-tinted print, were very popular in their day.*

RIGHT *It is odd to think that this beautifully decorated space was once a cow barn with a low ceiling for storing hay! With superb attention to detail, the end result is an impressive, comfortable and light-filled room — a tranquil haven for guests.*

Once work on the house had been completed, attention was turned to the barn, which sits across from the main house in front of the beautifully laid-out vegetable garden and the donkeys' paddock. The donkeys were an unusual but appropriate birthday gift – the owner grew up with donkeys and knows all too well how effective they are as lawnmowers!

The barn, traditionally used for animals and storing hay, is a simple structure, but one that he felt could be turned into a comfortable, self-contained dwelling for family and friends.

Although the barn contains just a bedroom, kitchen, bathroom and living room, they are all of generous proportions, and what the barn lacks in quantity of rooms is far outweighed by their charm.

Behind a fully glazed front door is a square space, not a hall as you might expect but a panelled kitchen painted a soft sage-green. Although most guests will probably trip over to the main house to partake of the owner's hospitality and delicious cooking, the kitchen is fully equipped. An English oak tilt-top table for dining is set in the middle of the terracotta-tiled floor. It makes an intimate dining space for two, perfect for a breakfast of eggs gathered from the hens that roam free outside the door as well as an elaborate supper, served on any one of

ABOVE LEFT *A large log basket sits beside one of a pair of English Gothic carved oak chairs. They make handsome as well as comfortable fireside chairs.*
FAR LEFT *This collection of old Bakelite switches was an unusual gift. For the time being, they make an interesting display on the bottom shelf of the Irish corner cupboard, but the intention is to one day restore and install them.*
LEFT *The handmade wooden model of Shandon Cathedral is a true replica of the present church built in 1722 in the city. The name Shandon comes from the Irish,* Sean Dun, *meaning 'old fort'. The cathedral is sited on one of Ireland's most famous Christian landmarks, and there has been a place of worship here since the 6th century.*

the many antique plates and platters stashed away in the 'press' (the Irish term for a cupboard).

The owner has amassed an impressive collection of Irish spongeware. There was a time, not so long ago, when this 18th-century vernacular pottery was not considered worth collecting, but it has enjoyed a recent renaissance. Increasingly hard to buy now, it commands prices that would cause its makers to die a second time round, laughing in their graves!

A large woven basket by Galway artist Joe Hogan reflects the multitude of natural colours used in the barn's decor and the vegetation outside. It is far too beautiful to be used for its intended purpose, so it hangs on the wall and is the first sight to greet you as you walk through the door.

ABOVE *The corner cupboard — another Irish vernacular piece of furniture, with the same two-tone colouring as the press in the kitchen — fits neatly into the available space. The scrubbed-top dining table, used as a side table, is also Irish. Propped up behind is a graphic but subtle contemporary painting on board. Past copies of* The World of Interiors *magazine, stacked in neat piles, are a bible for those with an interest in decoration.*

The bulk of the building is given over to one large room situated to the left of the kitchen. A pair of impressive, ornate Moroccan doors open onto this glorious space, with its steeply pitched roof, exposed white-painted beams and lime-washed walls. It is a peaceful space, lending itself to relaxation and repose, and is also incredibly comfortable. There's no television to intrude on

the perfect peace, just a neat little sound system with a small stack of carefully selected classical CDs. Warmth – always a high priority in Irish homes – is provided by a wood-burning stove, which forms the focus on the gable-end wall, and the thick curtains made from Irish tweed hanging at the sliding doors on either side of the room.

Throughout the barn, there is an eclectic mix of furniture. In the main room, a curvacious modern sofa sits comfortably alongside a pair of 19th-century Gothic Revival oak chairs and a Gothic side table. The decoration is also eclectic and undeniably masculine. Various decorative pieces, from a stuffed duck in a glass case and a huge pair of elk's antlers on top of the table to a handmade, wooden model of Shandon Cathedral

ABOVE *The only bedroom is a comfortable haven under the eaves. A pair of sturdy Irish kitchen chairs have been put into use as bedside tables. The antique map above the bed shows the province of Munster, into which County Cork falls.*
RIGHT *Reading by candlelight, although a romantic notion, is not good for the eyes. With that in mind, cleverly concealed lighting has been installed behind the beams.*

in Cork City, have been carefully chosen to complement each other. Dotted around the room are paintings by contemporary Irish artists.

The furniture that the owner treasures most of all are the Irish pieces, such as the glazed cupboard that has pride of place in the kitchen, and the corner cupboard and enormous painted Irish dresser, originally from a Dublin monastery, in the main room. Even though the dresser has been salvaged, stripped and repainted, it still retains its soul – some sentimental restorer has even left in place an old knife sharpener that was once crudely nailed to the work surface. Judging by its condition, it looks as though many blades have passed through it. Instead of being laden down with pots, pans and other kitchenware, as was originally intended, the dresser is now packed higgledy-piggledy with travel, cookery and art books. A particularly good read must surely be the paperback entitled *The Irish Donkey*!

A discreet panelled door off the kitchen leads to a compact shower room with lime-washed walls. Set into a bespoke unit, painted in Farrow & Ball's French Gray, is a neat, modern sink with a streamlined mixer tap/faucet. A small, glazed oak cupboard mounted on the wall is chock-a-block with pristinely folded fluffy white towels. Adding a vibrant touch to this soothing space is a jaunty striped kilim on the black-painted floorboards.

In a corner of the lime-washed kitchen, a wooden staircase, painted in a rich Etruscan red, leads up to a double bedroom tucked in beneath the eaves. Like the main room, this small space is quiet and peaceful, within earshot of the sound of the sea outside, which soon lulls you to sleep. The large bed is draped with a colourful patchwork bedspread that was brought back from Rajasthan.

ABOVE *The successful recipe of mixing the old with the new comes up trumps yet again in the shower room at the back of the kitchen. The influence of foreign travel is in evidence here, too, with a melange of multicultural objects on display, including an English carver chair, a dairy vessel from Eastern Europe used for holding loo rolls, a large sponge from a Greek island and a Moroccan pot and wall light.*

The beams immediately above the bed have been thoughtfully padded with fragments of an Indian carpet, to protect the head should you leap out of bed with a start at the morning chorus of braying donkeys just outside!

Elegant
IRISH

Arriving at this 19th-century fishing lodge on the shores of a lake puts one in mind of the opening lines of John McGahern's novel That They May Face The Rising Sun: *'The morning was clear. There was no wind on the lake. There was also a great stillness.'*

BY THE LAKE

By coincidence, McGahern's novel is a great favourite of the house's owner, an American who not only fell in love with this green isle, but also with one of its sons. The couple have owned this lakeside house for 20 years and have put their own distinctive mark on it.

There is a solidity to the house and outhouses that gives a reassuring sense of permanence and longevity, and so it comes as no surprise to discover that they are built on the site of a 13th-century castle. The handsome main building, constructed from coursed rubble stone, sits in a truly idyllic location, amid a landscape that has inspired poets and artists through the centuries.

The owners worked with an architect, a couple of designers, a gardener and various artists and artisans (one of whom built the stone walls around the property

RIGHT *Painted in a handsome Farrow & Ball green, lined with well-stocked bookcases and dimly lit with an open fire, the library is the heart and soul of the house. Within the confines of these dark walls, one is enveloped in the silence of a good book and the comfort of an old leather armchair. The only intrusion is the crackling of the flames.*

and can be found of an evening playing his accordion in the local bar) to realize their vision for the house. The glorious outside has been brought in, for every room has a view, and what a view at that! The architect, Richard Falconer, certainly fulfilled his brief.

The film *The Hours*, based on Virginia Woolf's novel *Mrs Dalloway*, inspired the owner's plans for the interior decoration. While she loved the Bloomsbury aesthetic, she didn't want to emulate the style of Charleston House, where Woolf's sister lived, and instead chose to draw inspiration from a rich but muted Bloomsbury palette.

LEFT *This tranquil scene is neither a painting nor a trompe l'oeil, but the stunning view from the front of the house!*

BELOW LEFT *A Victorian chest used as a side table in the family room displays the crackled patina of age. Originally a mail box, it used to travel to and from Dublin in a coach.*

BELOW *Irish blankets on the hall bench.*

OPPOSITE ABOVE *In the family room, a Victorian three-column pedestal table takes centre stage. It is covered with piles of books, each one weighed down with a single stone. The double doors leading to the garden are curtained with a thick Galway plaid.*

OPPOSITE BELOW *The stone floor in the entrance hall is softened with a large red rug.*

The interior marries this subtle colour scheme with a dash of clean-lined New England chic, the end result being a sophisticated yet welcoming country home.

Entering through the front door, one steps into an expansive main hall laid with warm grey French limestone flooring. This, in turn, leads onto a large, comfortable family room, its walls lined with nautical prints and maps. These were discovered rolled up and forgotten, but after taking the rocky road to Dublin, they returned framed and resplendent. Comfort is a priority here, and the sumptuous sofas and deep armchairs set

the tone for the rest of the interior. Most of the furniture was already in the house, having been bought locally over the years. Being of good quality, it was not replaced but either newly upholstered in fine traditional fabrics or sent off to the French polishers.

The spacious country-style kitchen is a cook's dream. With a large dresser painted in Farrow & Ball's subtle Powder Blue, it also boasts a walk-in pantry, a range cooker and all the gadgets one could possibly need, as well as an array of well-thumbed cookbooks – evidence that this kitchen is far from being just for display. There is a spacious breakfast room next door, home to a warming Aga and a painted pine Irish dresser. The American interior designer Tricia Foley, a long-standing family friend, was working for Wedgwood at the same time as her involvement with this house. She took advantage of staff discounts, filling her trunk, and subsequently the dresser, with elegant white bone china.

LEFT *In the breakfast room, the old Irish pine table, draped with a kilim, has space for eight rattan, ladder-back chairs plus two carvers. Barry's Tea, enjoyed everywhere in Ireland, is taken here in elegant mochaware mugs. This glazing technique originated in the 1780s in Staffordshire, with the dendritic, moss-like pattern achieved by using, among other substances, tobacco.*
ABOVE RIGHT *On the wall to the right of the large sash window is a print of a Shorthorn bull and his keeper. Portraits of livestock were popular during the 18th century.*
BELOW RIGHT *An unframed impressionistic oil on canvas leans against the dresser.*

For more formal occasions, the splendid dining room can be found just along the corridor. Taking centre stage here is the incredible shell-encrusted chandelier and a pair of matching candlesticks. These pieces were created by Diana Reynell, a shell artist who also worked on the restoration of the shell grotto at Hampton Court House. The simple Irish Victorian mahogany furniture has a glass-like sheen and is given an almost contemporary feel in this setting, partnered as it is with the modern

Irish paintings that the owners collect. Similarly, the modern William Yeoward glassware and original Georgian cut-glass decanters sit together harmoniously. The adjoining library is the heart and soul of the house. Painted in Farrow & Ball's Green Smoke and dimly lit with an open fire, the snug interior invites one to indulge in hours of luxurious reading.

When this house is filled with family, friends and visitors, as it so often is, there is a buzz of

enthusiasm for the many different activities on offer. If ever there was a place to inspire, this is it. For those tempted to try their hand with a paintbrush, a former cowshed has been transformed into an artists' studio, while for those in a more literary frame of mind there is a fairy-tale, waterside tower that has been cleverly converted from a grain silo into a writing room.

Surrounded by the many joys of this house, the words of the American essayist John Burroughs seem particularly apt: 'I still find each day too short for all the thoughts I want to think, all the walks I want to take, all the books I want to read, and all the friends I want to see.'

OPPOSITE PAGE *The dining room is painted a subtle greeny-blue with off-white woodwork. The large gilt overmantel mirror reflects the spectacular shell-encrusted chandelier.*
ABOVE, FROM LEFT TO RIGHT *A collection of antique silver ladles, a set of silver lustreware side plates and the ceiling rose of the shell chandelier all bring a sparkle to the room.*
RIGHT *A landscape by Alexander Mackenzie (1923–2002) takes centre stage over a Victorian mahogany sideboard.*

ABOVE *On the upstairs landing, this very good example of what is sometimes called a 'fool's chair' is a genuine Irish antique.*

LEFT *One of a pair of simple oak hall chairs sits in the main entrance hall, snugly tucked into a niche created by the curve of the staircase.*

ABOVE RIGHT *The large bathroom is comfortable and luxurious. The four-panelled screen can be moved around the room according to where privacy is required.*

BELOW RIGHT *Farrow & Ball's Cooking Apple Green is the chosen wall colour for the bedroom and bathroom. The blankets and carpet are of a similar subdued tone.*

BELOW LEFT *Prints and paintings of the Irish landscape hang each side of the king-sized bed.*

Dun Laoghaire is a beautiful Dublin suburb by the sea, a short drive from the city centre. It is also the main port where the ferry crosses the Irish Sea to Holyhead.

AMANDA'S NEST

The architecture here is predominantly Georgian, and the atmosphere genteel. The art galleries, chic flower shops and smart restaurants cater to an affluent population.

A street that gently slopes down to the sea is lined on one side with magnificent detached Regency villas. They are not numbered but, more elegantly, christened! The first house, tucked behind a large stone wall, is named Maplebury, after a mature tree in the garden. Built in 1835, Maplebury is where Amanda Pratt and her husband Tom Kelly, a creative director and film

ABOVE *Various trinkets, including an upper and a lower case 'A', decorate one of the white marble fireplaces in the drawing room.*
LEFT *The large double doors between the front and back drawing rooms on the first floor are always left open, allowing through swathes of natural light. The green container holding tulips reverts back to its original use as a coal bucket in winter.*

and media man, and their twin daughters Holly Star and Indigo have lived for the past 17 years.

A designer by profession, Amanda is the joint CEO and creative director of Avoca, one of Ireland's largest companies, employing over 600 staff. Avoca is a household name in Ireland, and one that is becoming increasingly known in the UK and abroad, too. The company started life in 1723 as a woollen mill in Avoca, County Wicklow, but fell on hard times. It was brought back to life by Amanda's entrepreneurial solicitor father Donald and her mother Hilary in the 1970s. Today it has a multimillion euro turnover.

The business is still very much a family concern, with Amanda, her three siblings and her parents continuing to run the show – one can imagine family get-togethers being exactly like a board meeting! Simon is the talent behind the Avoca kitchen. With an ethos of using Irish produce of the best quality and working with traditional methods, the kitchen produces the delicious food for the ten Avoca cafes and restaurants. Vanessa and Ivan look after the retail side and worldwide exports respectively, while Amanda is the head of the ever-growing fashion and design side of the Avoca business.

OPPOSITE *The red toile de Jouy wallpaper in the hall brings a distinctly French flavour to the space. It's a little-known fact that toile de Jouy, in production since the early 18th century, owes a great deal to an Irish inventor for its existence. Francis Nixon from Dublin discovered how to use engraved copperplates and a cylinder system to transfer design to cloth, which was much more cost-effective than wood-block printing.*

BELOW LEFT *Although the twins have now long grown out of these matching fluffy cream coats, bought when the girls were about five years old, they remain hanging in the hall as a reminder of their childhood.*

BELOW RIGHT *Just inside the back door in an alcove is an attractive little 19th-century French chair, sporting several pairs of Chinese silk slippers in lieu of upholstery!*

LEFT *This porter's chair dates from the mid–19th century and is upholstered in faded rose velvet. Originating in 16th–century France, porter's chairs were known as* guérites, *meaning 'sentry box'. They were used by hall porters as they kept watch at the doors of grand homes and palaces.*

When Amanda and Tom bought Maplebury in 1994, it was in fine condition, having never been subjected to the Philistine removal of its original splendid fireplaces or inappropriate replacement windows. It is altogether an imposing house, set on a slight slope and with the upstairs rooms looking out to a view of the sea. The side entrance, which would originally have been for tradesmen and staff, is the door that everyone uses these days instead of the formal front door at the front of the house. This down-to-earth attitude sums up this hard-working family – no one has any apparent airs and graces, and everyone mucks in together.

The house is furnished quite modestly and with a muted palette, but vibrancy is provided by bold splashes of colour from paintings and flowers. The entrance hallway is perhaps the most ornate room in terms of decoration, with pretty red toile de Jouy wallpaper hung below the dado rail. In contrast, the downstairs bathroom is almost Shaker-like in its austerity, with simple white tongue-and-groove panelling and no unnecessary ornamentation. But, just for fun, the zinc letters 'W A S H', resting on the ledge of the elbow-height panelling, leave no one in any doubt about the room's purpose!

THIS PAGE *The silk jacket hanging above the mantelpiece was originally made for Amanda's great grandmother, Maude. A sepia photograph on the mantelpiece below shows Maude on her wedding day in about 1870 wearing the very same jacket. The ornamental bonsai tree is made of rose quartz.*
OPPOSITE RIGHT *One of the perks of the job is bringing home the stock, such as these woollen throws!*

Moving down the hall, a colourful light-filled room has become the twins' workroom. They each have their own desks but, after swotting for exams or doing their homework, there is a bright, comfortable arrangement of four chairs around a coffee table from Senegal for relaxing.

On the other side of the hall is the dining room, which leads into an open-plan, modern kitchen and utility space. The panelled bay window, with fitted wooden seats, made comfortable with a jamboree of cushions, and a small round pedestal table, is the perfect spot for

BELOW LEFT *The reviews of the various incarnations of the Avoca Cafe Cookbook have been glowing. If they are good enough for the great Irish public, then they are certainly good enough for the cook in this household! A freshly picked bunch of rosemary from the garden makes an attractive, if prickly, posy alongside a single perfect pink camellia.*

BELOW RIGHT *This Is Just To Say, this is just a plum!*

Instead of a formal dining room, this large, happy space, which is the eating end of the kitchen, is bright, airy and uncluttered.

The vibrant colours in this child's painting perfectly complement the pink and blue of the extra kitchen chairs.

drinking tea and reading the *Irish Times*. Taking centre stage is the scrubbed pine table, with brightly gloss-painted Victorian kitchen chairs. Lively family meals are enjoyed here. Tom is head of the kitchen, which is just as well because Amanda isn't interested in cooking. She much prefers designing at the kitchen table or collecting eggs from her hens – a recent birthday gift.

Admired by all are the two vibrant paintings on the wall. Amanda chuckles when she admits one was painted by the twins when they were young, and the other she did herself when she was in urgent need of some 'Art' for the opening of another Avoca cafe – she bought a pile of canvasses and had great fun sloshing paint around on the kitchen floor. Just a trace of the original kitchen

RIGHT *A large glass jar, which would originally have been used for home-brewing, is now a penny or, more correctly, a cent jar, while a pottery pudding basin has become a vase for a white hydrangea. A pretty French chest of drawers of no great age or worth has been newly painted and provides useful storage.*
BELOW *Tea always tastes better from a china cup!*

remains: a little window above the sink. Above that is a shelf housing a lovely collection of vases, glass bottles and zinc buckets, used for the fresh flowers that are Amanda's little luxury.

To match the wallpaper in the hall, the sweeping staircase is carpeted in red and leads upstairs to an elegant, high-ceilinged and parquet-floored double drawing room. Both sides have identical functioning fireplaces, complete with the original baskets and white marble surrounds. These support unframed family photographs, vases of flowers, fairy lights and various mementoes and souvenirs of far-flung travels.

One end of the room is book-lined and home to a deep, comfortable modern sofa, where everyone can flop in front of an unconcealed, large-screen television. The opposite end of the room is more formal, although comfort has not been compromised. There are another two sofas, as well as a French upholstered porter's chair, but that most definitely is not for slouching in! Where there are no bookshelves, the painted

RIGHT *The glazed door into the white kitchen allows in the maximum amount of natural light. A traditional and utilitarian space, the kitchen nonetheless has a softness to it, created by fabrics with just a hint of floral pattern.*

BELOW *Peeping through the internal scullery window, you can see a tall wooden rack with sliding shelves for storing vegetables and fruit. The piece of wicker that looks like a beehive is for storing potatoes.*

ABOVE *The furnishings in the main bedroom are a complete melange of styles, effortlessly put together to create a dreamy and tranquil effect. Reflected in the wall-mounted mirror is a huge, contemporary painted four-poster bed. The Victorian chest of drawers and the Edwardian washstand, with its pretty tiled back, have both been given a face lift with a coat of powder-blue paint. Adding a touch of glamour to the scene is the 19th-century French gilt wood chair covered in a soft pink satin fabric.*

LEFT *It's fun to use furniture and objects out of context. Here, in the downstairs bathroom, there is a slatted garden chair and a square, folding metal bistro table.*
BELOW *A dainty pile of Avoca's own soaps.*

embossed wallpaper shows through. Everywhere there are piles of colour-coordinated throws, shawls and blankets; the trademark of Avoca.

The teenagers' interconnecting bedrooms are vibrant and colourful, just as they should be. In contrast, the master bedroom, carpeted and with a simple painted four-poster bed, is understated and unadorned, except for a collection of mementoes and love tokens on the wall above the bed, reminiscent of 19th-century prayer votives.

Amanda's love of letters and fonts (she always wears a tiny 'A' around her neck) is in further evidence in the bedroom – there is a large 'A' on her dressing table and a little one lives at her bedside. 'A' is for Amanda, 'A' is for Avoca...

OPPOSITE BELOW LEFT *Seen up close are some of the trinkets and treasured mementoes that Amanda and her husband have collected over the years and which now hang on the wall over the bed. The item mounted like an 'X' is actually a pair of antique cut-steel hair grips. Jewellery made of cut steel first came into fashion in the mid-1700s. It was orginally manufactured out of recycled horseshoe nails in England and became very popular in France. It then came to be made of faceted rosettes of polished steel set in an intricate design. Cut-steel jewellery is now extremely collectable.*

OPPOSITE BELOW RIGHT *Continuing the decorative theme of the letter 'A' found throughout the house, a lower-case initial in an extra-bold font, made of wood and covered with a printed pattern reminiscent of silver birch bark, is propped up against the backdrop of tiles on the washstand in the main bedroom.*

Ballybrittan Castle is an extended tower house, and although the tower is now in a ruinous state, the place is still known as a castle.

OFFALY GRAND

Situated in County Offaly in the province of Leinster (the largest province in Ireland), Ballybrittan dates from the 15th century and is a rare example of an Irish vernacular building believed to have been a place of continuous habitation for a thousand years or more.

The castle featured in many military entanglements during the 16th and 17th centuries, ownership passing from pillar to post, until around 1700 when it was leased to the Inman family, one of the pioneering Quaker families in Ireland. Fast-forward to 1998, when a Dublin couple bought the property, which ultimately became a new home for them and their four children.

The house, with its white-painted façade, stands at right angles to the tower. It was probably built at the start of the 18th century and has the appearance of a long, five-bay, gable-ended house. The 'new' entrance hall was added in 1720. Set in the middle of the house, it features a tessellated tiled floor that is distinctly Victorian in its excessive decoration. The tiles are toned down by the almost austere decor, which allows the elegant, early 18th-century wooden staircase, painted in Farrow & Ball's Bone, to stand out resplendently

against the walls, which are painted in Farrow & Ball's Hardwick White. There is nothing in the hall other than three oak chairs – to clutter this entrance would not respect its elegance. The panelled door at the far end leads to a back hallway that holds jackets, coats, boots and shoes.

Most of the fine joinery and panelling in the house is original, and over the course of two years, soon after the family moved in, the owners had it meticulously restored. During the course of the

ABOVE *A perfectly manicured lawn and a low-cut box hedge do nothing to interfere with the simple lines of this period house.*
RIGHT *The murals in the airy dining room are by the celebrated contemporary artist Michael Dillon and are reminiscent of Giovanni Panini's fanciful vistas of Roman antiquities. The murals depict follies dotted over an 18th-century landscape, in which classical ruins are erected at various identifiable locations around Ballybrittan Castle. All the structures come from a sort of imaginary salvage yard full of recovered columns, pediments and urns, but instead of traditional acanthus leaves and the like, Michael has painted oak and beech leaves, from the trees at Ballybrittan. On the circular table, a classical figure of Aphrodite, or Venus, the goddess of love and beauty, shares the limelight with the glorious murals.*

OPPOSITE *Tessellation, a repeating mosaic pattern of small interlocking shapes, usually of glazed clay, occurs throughout history, from ancient architecture to modern art. Seen here in the entrance hall is a magnificent Victorian example of a tessellated tiled floor. The cornicing is simple and severe, allowing the flamboyant ceiling rose to stand out. Suspended from its centre is a reproduction brass lantern.*

restoration work, an old oak window surround dating from the Tudor period was discovered in the hall. Very few such wooden window surrounds are still surviving in Ireland.

By his very nature, the man of the house is fascinated by such detail. Animated and informed, he proudly and enthusiastically tells stories of the house and its history. When describing the dining room, on the left of the hall, he tells how the acclaimed mural artist Michael Dillon, whose work can be seen at Fortnum & Mason on Piccadilly (London), was asked to transform this room into the fantasy it now is. While residing in the house, this 'gentleman painter' completely charmed the housekeeper, who kept him constantly supplied with great mugs of tea! The restrained elegance of the 19th-century Irish mahogany hunt table is in sober contrast to the decorative frivolity of the room in which it stands. Having been treated with reverence all its life, it has a mirror-like sheen.

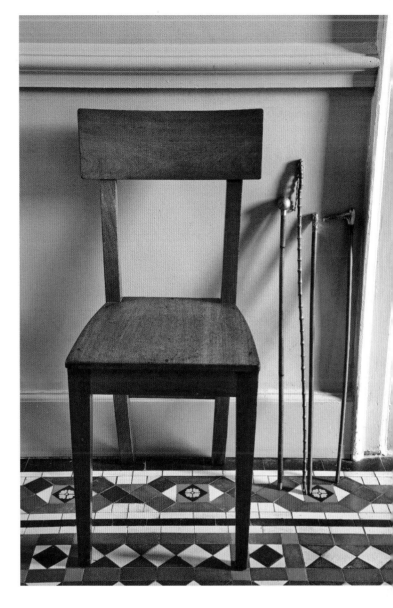

ABOVE LEFT *On the inside of the front door, this gargantuan old surface-mounted lock, complete with an equally enormous key, is in full working order. Securing one's property is an age-old concern. Historians have suggested that there is evidence of use of locking mechanisms dating back to early Roman civilization.*
ABOVE RIGHT *One of a pair of perfectly simple oak hall chairs fits neatly beneath the dado rail in the hall. To one side stands a collection of delicate canes. These are not in fact walking canes, but rather a selection of canes that would have been used in the showing of horses (at agricultural shows, horse shows and the like), including a very elegant lady's riding cane.*

LEFT *A large silver meat dome is engraved with the letter 'J', for the owner's name. The ancient stone arch behind it, now filled in with old bricks, was once either a door or passageway that led to the castle.*

To the right of the hall is the library. The walls, painted in Farrow & Ball's Drab, benefit from three large, six-over-six sash windows. With their shutters permanently open, as much natural light as possible floods in. The sobriety and elegance of the furnishings and the four matching 19th-century English Gothic Revival leather chairs lend themselves to happy hours of reading. The shelves are packed tightly with books on every conceivable subject in Gaelic and English by writers as diverse as Tomás Ó Criomhthain to Molly Keane and William Trevor.

In 1859, the American educational reformer Horace Mann wrote that 'Books are the window through which the soul looks out... A house without books is like a room without windows. No man has a right to bring up his children without surrounding them with books, if he has the means to buy them.' The four children in this family are

ABOVE *A pair of French doors in the kitchen are kept permanently shut to allow for an extra work area. The modern kitchen chairs are in homage to a traditional design and are similar to the chairs in the hall.*
LEFT *A mahogany tray holds silver forks, spoons and bone-handled steel knives.*

OPPOSITE *The 18th-century mahogany carver with a pierced splat provides an ample seat in the rear entrance hall to pull on a fine pair of leather riding boots. The slim gilt Georgian mirror with a classical frieze has an original mercury plate, but it's not so foxed that you can't see if your hat is on straight! Three blue and white platters are displayed in descending size on the wall.*

LEFT *An invite to the Cork Film Festival sits on the wooden mantelpiece in the well-stocked library. Established in 1956, the festival is one of Ireland's premier cultural events, drawing local, national and international interest.*

fortunate to have been brought up in such an enlightened home. It is blessed with many windows, but even more books. There isn't a room in the house that doesn't have piles of them – even the kitchen is no exception. The main book buyer is the children's father, who is to be seen several times a week in Hodges Figgis, his favourite bookshop in Dublin and which, he proclaims, is the finest bookshop in the world, no less. In return, he is probably one of their best customers!

The galley kitchen, with its terracotta-tiled floor, was designed by Clive Nunn from Thomastown in County Kilkenny. A well-balanced mixture of the traditional and the modern, it contains bespoke fitted cupboards and a wall-mounted plate rack by Hans Leptien, based in Cork, as well as an antique pine washstand used to store all the equipment needed for baking. What makes this kitchen truly unique, though,

LEFT *If there is any truth in the saying, 'The closest we will ever come to an orderly universe is a good library', then the proportions of this elegant library, with its sash windows on three sides, are as near as you will find to perfection. The shelves are crammed with books and the walls lined with engravings and prints, while the antique chairs proffer comfort to read at leisure.*

ABOVE *The elegant, fluid lines of this 19th-century mahogany drop-leaf table are not diminished by the simple white china wash bowl placed upon it. The bowl would originally have been partnered with a matching pitcher.*

RIGHT *A sofa table in the drawing room gives succour to an unlikely arrangement of objects: the resin head of a Buddha, a pair of Irish silver candlesticks in the classical style and, on top of a pile of leather-bound books, a pair of stainless-steel gynaecological forceps — tools of the trade belonging to the lady of the house but no longer in use!*

is the primitive stone arch, filled in with more recent haphazard brickwork – evidence of a door or passageway that would have led to the castle.

Beside the kitchen, another staircase, carpeted in blue, leads the way to the upstairs drawing room, which is lined with stunning, late 17th-century Baltic pine panelling. A visiting member of the Irish Georgian society stoked an interesting debate as to whether it should be covered in fabric, as would have been originally intended. Until a consensus is reached, it remains untouched.

PREVIOUS SPREAD *The guest bedroom and bathroom ooze atmosphere and are redolent of another age, despite enjoying the very 21st-century luxuries of central heating and permanent hot and cold running water. Taking centre stage in the bedroom is the wooden four-poster bed, its heavy red velvet curtains lined with a sage-green glazed cotton. It is not unusual to see such a plain fireplace in a bedroom of a house from this period, and its lack of ornamentation does not detract from its robust handsomeness. Unlike its neighbour in the bathroom, this fireplace is still in use. The bedroom panelling and the window casement in the bathroom have both been restored sympathetically and sensitively. The scarlet upholstery of the Victorian balloon back chair in the bathroom provides a splash of vibrant colour against the elegant teal-blue painted walls.*

Decorating the drawing room walls is a varied collection of framed prints, engravings and artworks, including an important watercolour of Ballybrittan Castle by the 19th-century Irish architect and watercolourist Sandham Symes, which was once in the collection of the Knight of Glin. Everything about this room is refined and elegant, from the rich green damask upholstery on all the seating to the sumptuous burgundy raw silk curtains with contrasting eau de Nil lining.

It's hard to drag yourself away from an alluring turf fire on a winter's evening, but it's not such a hardship in this house, as all the bedrooms have functioning fireplaces. But even when the fires

aren't lit, the panelling in the bedrooms – painted in Farrow & Ball's Green Smoke in the master bedroom and Chappell Green in the guest room – is comforting and warm in tone. These are the two most beautiful bedrooms in the house, both with four-poster beds and their own bathrooms, each with reproduction antique baths.

Over the years, the present owners have restored this historic house with the utmost care and, at the same time, have made it into an elegant but comfortable home. They have more than done justice to the unique monument in their care and take enormous pride in sharing the tales of its distant past with others.

OPPOSITE ABOVE *The master bedroom has a more contemporary feel than the guest bedroom, with a modern take on the four-poster. A French gilt Louis XVI sofa stands at the end of the bed, adding a touch of glamour to the room. The displays of wall-mounted blue and white platters and framed prints above the bedside tables are almost symmetrical, while above the fireplace, either side of the artwork by Maria Simonds-Gooding, the symmetry is repeated but this time more rigorously.*

ABOVE LEFT *The bathroom boasts its original panelling. The rug breaks up the expanse of wooden flooring and provides comfort.*

ABOVE RIGHT *The newel posts, spindles and banisters of the main staircase are in such pristine condition that you could be fooled into believing that they are replacements, but the staircase is completely original and dates back to the early 18th century.*

With a maiden name of Ireland, it seems almost preordained that London–born Mary Jane Russell would end up making her home there, just outside the ancient city of Cork.

IRELAND'S OWN

'Heaven indeed had provided the location for their house, which overlooked a lovely bit of the Blackwater with green fields beyond, and flanking these were heather-covered mountains… and over all hung the soft haze of the long Irish twilight… It was a perfect country home.'

Although these anonymous words were written back in 1936, nothing much has changed when it comes to a description of the 'perfect country home', and this fine Georgian house certainly ticks all the boxes. The house dates from 1770 and is situated about 28 miles outside Cork, Ireland's second-largest city. Its present owners came to view it after they had divided up and sold a large family estate nearer to the city. Invisible from the road, with a southerly aspect, superb views and not too

much land to maintain, this house suited them down to the ground. And, best of all, it was the most inexpensive house they had viewed, as it needed a massive decorative makeover.

Philip Russell, a native Cork man, met his London-born wife Mary Jane in England, where he had been at school. At her boarding school in Cirencester, she'd made lots of Irish friends, so it wasn't altogether surprising that she eventually fell for the charms of one of their friends who happened to be Irish!

In 1996, after having two of her three children, Mary Jane opened her interiors shop, Town and Country, in Cork city. This quickly became a successful and flourishing concern and, in 2009, she transferred the business to her home,

LEFT *A corner of the fine Irish white marble fireplace in the entrance hall shows in detail the intricate 'tooth' motif, decorative carvings and inlays of grey relief.*
OPPOSITE *What was originally the main front door of the house before the Victorian porch extension was added is pure Georgian. It is seen here ajar, opening inwards to the large entrance hall, with its comfortable sisal carpeting and a huge patterned rug on top. One of a pair of caned–back hall chairs sits beneath the portrait of an ancestor in an ornate gilt frame. Large baskets of cut branches from the garden provide immediate sculptural, as well as completely gratis, displays.*

LEFT *The fireplace is home to an ornate antique bronze mantel clock, a family heirloom that has now ceased to tell the time. It is flanked by a large pair of faux urns and a modern pair of glass and silver hurricane lanterns.*

knocking together two bedrooms in the west wing of the house to create a generous work space for herself. Here, there are literally hundreds of fabric books – the tools of her trade. Unsurprisingly, Mary Jane uses the designs of her sister, the California-based textile and fabric designer Kathryn Ireland, whenever she can.

A self-taught interior decorator, Mary Jane was undaunted by the task of transforming the five-bedroom house into a beautiful and comfortable home for her and Philip, their children and their two dogs. Meanwhile, Philip, who had studied estate management, turned his expertise to the grounds and gardens.

The breakfront, pebble-dashed house is reached by a tree-lined, gravel drive. A porch, added during Victorian times, has a tall, arched window, setting it apart from the other nine sash windows, which are faithful to the original architecture. Although not in keeping with the Georgian architecture, the porch does offer protection from the elements, especially as the front door opens into the huge entrance hall.

The right side of the hall is used as a drawing room. An elegant, sweeping staircase in the middle of the room faces the front door and,

The large entrance hall is now used as a
comfortable drawing room. The term
'drawing' derives from the 16th century, when
the room was used by the owners of the house
for 'withdrawing' for privacy. These days, the
drawing room is more often referred to as
the living room. The walls are Farrow & Ball's
Joa's White, with blue the accent colour in the
damask curtains, soft furnishings and even in
the large painting on the wall.

although it is not original to the house, its fine joinery and styling, as well as excellent paintwork, would certainly fool the Irish Georgian Society! At the foot of the stairs, an atmospheric modern canvas that Mary Jane bought from London art dealer Sophie Montgomery suits the large expanse of wall perfectly.

The beautiful white marble Irish fireplace, which Mary Jane found in the nearby town of Youghal, forms the backdrop to a wood-burning stove that throws out heat all winter. A mixture of contemporary and antique seating enforces Mary Jane's trademark style of comfort combined with elegance.

To the left of the staircase, hanging above a scalloped, veneered Irish mahogany table, is an unusual, grandiose gilt and painted overmantel mirror. This treasured family heirloom, which belonged to Philip's father, came from Bunratty Castle in County Clare, where he was

brought up. The inset portrait of a lady in blue is an ancestor, while the sconces either side of the mirror were added recently. Flanking the table is a pair of carved oak hall chairs with caned backs and canvas seats. Even though these pieces are of completely different styles, together they make a most interesting, if unexpected, arrangement.

As in all the best homes, the kitchen is the hub. Traditional but with a contemporary twist, this kitchen was designed by Mary Jane, then built by Sasha Whelan of the Allen family from nearby Ballymaloe House. The matt powdery blue units, painted in Farrow & Ball's Parma Gray, have glossy teak worktops, while the walls are Farrow & Ball's Off-White. Forming the central focus of the room is the Aga. This iconic kitchen range is an

ABOVE *The dining room and kitchen are divided by another wide archway, at which point the carpeting gives way to more practical flagstone flooring. This gives the room a traditional feel in spite of its modern fittings.*

OPPOSITE ABOVE *The caning in this oak-framed hall chair is in excellent condition. Practised for centuries, the craft of caning is still a highly valued skill.*

OPPOSITE BELOW *Seen through an archway in the corner of the large hall is a passageway with an elegant William IV commode with claw feet. Originally from Cork, it is a fine example of such a piece of furniture. The pair of Victorian cut-glass decanters upon it hint at its use as a drinks cupboard. The simply decorated dining room is painted in the same Farrow & Ball Off-White. When the table is not in use, a pair of metal pomegranate sculptures sit in pride of place. Although intended as garden decorations, they look just as good inside as out.*

ABOVE *In the bathroom, a chrome towel rail from France, reminiscent of a luggage rack, holds a stack of unused white towels and also provides hooks for those in use.*
LEFT *The main staircase is uncarpeted and painted with hard-wearing floor paint. The mid-landing is deep enough to allow a Georgian tripod table to sit comfortably and show off the doll's house that was given to Mary Jane's daughter by her granny. Daylight is unrestricted by any drapes at the enormous sash window, but a large lantern from Vaughan provides light in the hours of darkness.*

integrated model, which means that it has an additional hob and oven that are independently fuelled for use during the warmer months, when constant heat from the main oven is not needed. A huge island in front is a multifunctional space that's used for family breakfasts, food preparation, flower arranging, afternoon tea, homework and a great deal more besides.

Positioned just to the right of a deep-set, six-over-six sash window, with a Kathryn Ireland print Roman blind, is a simple Georgian oak table supporting a large terracotta milk bowl. On the wall above is a charming drawing by the English artist Nigel Waymouth of Mary Jane and Philip's son Robin, when he was three years old.

A variety of traditionally crafted baskets, all made in Ireland, and a large collection of

ABOVE *The half-height wooden panelling provides a useful shelf below a Regency triptych overmantel. Combining the antique with the modern works particularly well in a bathroom, where there needs to be a balance between beauty and practicality. Two sinks have been set into a black granite surface on a hardwood frame. Deep baskets below contain all the clutter that would otherwise detract from the elegance of the room.*

Irishware, displayed on the open shelves in the kitchen, are all in frequent use. Many of these pieces were made by Nicholas Mosse, one of Ireland's best-known and most popular potteries, which is based in Kilkenny. Nicholas's mission was to produce beautiful, functional pottery in the style of Irish spongeware, which was the vernacular pottery of 18th-century Ireland. Spongeware was generally made in simple, practical forms with the

RIGHT *The long upstairs landing, off which all the bedrooms lead, has a magnificent view. In the middle of the hall, against the banister, is a glass-top showcase with drawers. On top sits a family heirloom — a bent steering wheel from a Lotus owned by Mary Jane's uncle, Robert McGregor Innes Ireland, which he crashed in a Formula One race in Monte Carlo in the 1950s.*

decoration applied with a cut sponge, hence the name. Even today, Mosse pottery is still made in exactly the same traditional way.

The simple dining room, which is adjacent to the kitchen, is home to a large and utilitarian, mahogany table surrounded by soft grey- and raspberry-coloured Lloyd Loom woven chairs – Mary Jane used to sell these in her shop. As with a number of rooms in the house, the windows, which all overlook the garden, are left bare to allow the light to flow in unrestricted.

Reached from the sweeping painted staircase in the main entrance hall, the upstairs rooms lead off a long, light, kilim-lined landing. The five bedrooms are all generously proportioned and command breathtaking views over the surrounding countryside. Like the other rooms in the house, the master bedroom is decorated in a palette of soothing, neutral shades. A Julian Chichester silk-screen print of a lurcher in a Plexiglass frame hangs above the French cane bed, introducing a bold and whimsical splash of colour.

In the bathroom, a rustic Irish butcher's block has been turned into a sturdy stool and sits beneath a chrome towel rack. This is reflected in an elegant Regency triptych-style gilt mirror that hangs on the opposite wall, creating a harmonious, if unlikely, pairing. Taking centre stage, though, is the pristine roll-top bath positioned just beneath the large sash window. Here, at the end of a busy day running her home and her business, Mary Jane can bathe contentedly in the 'soft haze of the long Irish twilight'.

ABOVE *In the tranquil master bedroom, the now-familiar theme of muted tones continues, with a deep sky-blue the colour of choice in the detail. The king-sized, painted caned bed is a reproduction piece and is draped with a hand-quilted cotton spread. An Irish rocking chair sits in front of the window, beside a large Victorian mahogany cheval glass, or dressing mirror. Originating from France in the 1700s, a cheval (French for horse) mirror is so-called because the sturdy base on which the actual mirror sits is known as a horse. To the right of the large sash window is a campaign chest of drawers, above which hangs a bleached shark's jawbone — a quirky decorative touch.*

Eclectic
IRISH

The novelist Elizabeth Bowen wrote 'owning a big house in Ireland is something between a predicament and a raison d'être'. Tad Christopher Wilbur, who lives at Red Hill with his daughter Grace, can testify to this.

'AN EXCELLENT HOUSE'

A privileged American brought up on a gilded surfboard in Honolulu, Tad moved to Ireland in 1999. With his young bride Tara and their baby daughter Grace, he settled at Red Hill, situated at the end of a lane in rural Sligo – a far cry from the catwalks of the world's fashion capitals, where Tad had once paraded as a model.

Built of rubble and yellow brick, then rendered, and with rusticated cut-limestone window and door surrounds, Red Hill was the creation of a Mr Andrew Baker, employed by the Marquis of Rockingham as a rent collector and solicitor, and who claimed to have built 'an excellent house' between 1832 and 1838. Mr Matthew Callaghan, a 98-year-old neighbour whose

grandfather worked on the building of the house, states in no uncertain terms that Mr Baker had the house built and then went to America for seven years while the statute of limitations period expired, to avoid having to pay for its construction!

When Tad and Tara came to Red Hill, they were passionate about bringing the Palladian-style mansion to life again, but it was a huge undertaking. The six-over-six Georgian sliding sash windows of cylinder glass had been smashed, the kitchen was a cattle shed, the entrance gates had been stolen and the fanlight over the front door was missing, too. There was no heating or modern plumbing. Parts of the roof needed replacing, and the grand staircase needed major restoration.

Red Hill is comprised of no less than 13 rooms. On the ground floor is the drawing room, dining room, study, kitchen, a large butler's pantry and two further pantries. A grand staircase leads up from the large central hall. Off the half-landing is a secondary staircase leading to the west wing. Here, a box room and a clothes and linen drying room have been turned into a bathroom and sitting room respectively. Also off the half-landing is the former 'Delft' room, once used for storing china but now converted into an additional bathroom.

The upstairs landing leads to five bedrooms, complete with their original Regency fireplaces. Incredibly, the house still has 11 such fireplaces,

RIGHT *A professional bottle opener in the pantry has clearly been put to good use!*
BELOW LEFT *Tucked in by the kitchen fireplace is a Boston rocker made by the Pennysylvania Dutch.*
BELOW RIGHT *The window ledge above the sink has a collection of unpolished brass candlesticks.*

OPPOSITE ABOVE *Traditional in style, the new Irish dresser in the kitchen has never been painted. Irish dressers are distinct from their English and Welsh cousins, being made in one solid piece rather than as a base with a separate top.*
OPPOSITE BELOW *This elegantly curvacious Dutch, six-branch brass chandelier is a far cry from the sides of meat that would have originally hung from the metal hooks dotted all over the kitchen ceiling.*

some of them with their original fireplace furniture. Together with the well-worn flagstone floors, the original inlaid doors, window surrounds and shutters, not to mention a brass bell system, which could, with a little attention, be restored to working order, these features all add up to a house awash with history and atmosphere.

While Red Hill is still standing, and will be, hopefully, for centuries to come (it is now on the Record of Protected Structures), sadly the marriage was not to last, and many of Tad's plans to return the house to its former glory were dashed. Red Hill is an example of true decaying grandeur. There is peeling paint everywhere, and the biscuit plaster walls in the main hall are a perfect example of what faux paint specialists try to re-create. The telephone is an old Bakelite model, securely fixed to the wall. Like the peeling paint, the unpolished floorboards may not be to everyone's taste, but they must be given some regard – after all, they have lasted 175 years.

ABOVE LEFT *The Sacred Heart, to be found in all good Irish Catholic homes, watches over the fine Collard & Collard pianoforte in the hallway.*

FAR LEFT *On the music room mantelpiece is a pair of china Irish setters sitting in the shade of a branch of a Chinese glass tree. The Gaelic name for these hunting dogs is* Madra rua, *meaning 'red dog'.*

LEFT *At the other end of the mantelpiece, alongside a decanter of peacock feathers and part of an old violin case, is a third edition of a humorous 19th-century book entitled* Life in Ireland.

The drawing of Tad that hangs over
the fireplace was done by the artist
Caspar Hall in 1996. It is in this
room, originally the main drawing
room and now the music room, that
Tad has composed some 86 songs,
including 'Lunasa, Festival Song',
which is on its way to becoming
a classic in Irish music circles.

The image of a harp is
synonymous with Ireland.
This ancient folk instrument,
with its ethereal sound, sits
on the landing, framed by
tattered curtains.

A small room on the top landing serves as Tad's study, where, among the paperwork, he stores some of the period costumes he has collected.

The drawing room still has its original Regency fire surround, although the grate is burned out. The only furnishing is a Victorian show-wood armchair, with its springs poking through. This room is now outfitted with recording equipment and an extensive collection of musical instruments. Music has always been a big part of life at Red Hill. The renowned flautist and fiddler Peter Horan informed Tad that Michael Coleman, a master of Irish fiddle music, often played here, and that the legendary Bothy Band once used the house to practise in. 'The Flowers of Red Hill', a lively, local reel, eulogizes the gardens, while 'The Man from Mullaghroe' is a slower air written some time in the last century about the house's original owner, Andrew Baker.

Red Hill seems as if it was designed for music – one player on the landing can fill all 13 rooms with music – and nowadays it still has an important role here. If you happen to be driving down a country lane in this part of Ireland late one night and catch a boogie riff emanating from a Georgian mansion atop a hill, it could very well be Tad playing the piano. On the other hand, it may just be the pixies and the fairies at their usual *craic*…

BELOW *The traces of original green paint on the walls in this unique bathroom were revealed after stripping away dozens of layers of old wallpaper. An antique bath with a wooden surround has been installed in the perfect position for bathers to take in the view. The impressive embossed copper pillar concealing the Aga flue and the copper door were specially made by Travellers.*

RIGHT *The unpainted pine staircase acts as a room divider and a convenient place for Jessy, the neighbour's cat, to peer out of the window. It's also somewhere to display favourite pairs of vintage brown leather shoes.*

West Cork has its own distinctive vibe, welcoming strangers and 'blow-ins', although Bernadette and Mick prefer to think of themselves as 'blow-backs!'

WHERE THE SUN ALWAYS SHINES

Ireland is littered with bungalows. Driving through any of the 26 counties, you will come across ruined stone farmhouses and cottages frequently sharing their plot of land with one of these obtrusive new structures. The mass emigration of young men and women from Ireland in the 1940s and '50s saw some of them returning home a number of years later, having made good abroad. Instead of lovingly restoring existing buildings that represented old Ireland, many built new homes. Too sentimental, though, to knock the original places down, they left them standing as a reminder of their origins.

LEFT *The child of post-war parents, Bernadette has a make-do-and-mend ethos. Her comfortable and cottagey living room contains an assortment of much-loved old seating. Blankets, throws and rugs cover up a multitude of sins, as well as adding an ethnic splash of colour and providing extra warmth.*

LEFT *The chunky antique brass kitchen taps/faucets, originally intended for a bathtub, and the unusual slate kitchen sink were the features that actually persuaded Bernadette and Mick to buy the house!*

Most of these bungalows are out of keeping with the landscape but, on the Mizen Peninsula in County Cork, one enlightened builder developed a clutch of inspirational dwellings. Blending in with their surroundings and built using traditional methods and materials, these cottages also have good eco credentials. It is in one of these that Bernadette O'Shea and Michael (Mick) Regan chose to make their home.

Born in England to a Kerry father and a Galway mother, Bernadette was educated at a Dominican convent in London. It was here, when she was 13, that she met Michael, of Kilkenny and Cork stock.

RIGHT *In the cosy cottage-style kitchen, kitchenware and mementoes crowd the shelves. Lest you not be tempted by the delicious smell of Bernadette's homemade scones and fresh soda bread, a vintage, hand-drawn placard declaims, in no uncertain terms, 'Eat More Bread'! A huge wooden cross, which originally came from a chapel in Berkshire, is attached to the ceiling beams above the kitchen table, as it was too big to fit anywhere else.*

The slogan on the kitchen blackboard grew out of Bernadette texting the local radio station as a way of putting Ballydehob on the map. Whenever the presenter gave his weather reports, come hell or high water, the sun always seemed to be shining in Ballydehob! The slogan became part of his jingle, then a logo for the village, and can now be seen on postcards and t-shirts on sale in the local post office.

Ballydehob....
Where the
Sun always shines!

ABOVE LEFT *Cherished shiny trinkets, including a vintage evening bag and a pair of dancing shoes sitting among 1930s canisters, are displayed on a kitchen cabinet.*

ABOVE RIGHT *Above the tea and coffee press is the 'family silver', where a picture of St Martin de Porres (1579–1639) leans against a three-branch pewter candlestick.*

On leaving school, the pair went their separate ways, Mick to follow a career in project management, and Bernadette to work in the world of interiors, theatre and photography. Now fast-forward 25 years, to when the internet brought our protagonists together again via the Friends Reunited website. Two more different people you cannot imagine, but the twinkle in their eyes and their shared past saw a teenage infatuation develop into two souls finding their mates.

Many years of travelling back and forth to Ireland visiting family tied Bernadette and Mick inextricably to the place. This, combined with the dream of living the rural idyll and the deep-seated notion that the children of the Irish diaspora were always expected to come 'home', led them

suddenly, and quite instinctively, in 2005 to take a leap of faith and move to Ireland. Mick saw the cottage they now live in online on a Tuesday, they viewed it the following day and put a deposit down on the Thursday. Four months later, they loaded a van with all their worldly goods and bought a one-way ticket on the Swansea to Cork ferry, en route for their new home in Ballydehob, a village on the Mizen Peninsula in West Cork.

Their cottage stands in the shadow of Mounts Corin and Gabriel, on a plot that is part-woodland and bound by two streams. The 'aged' stone cladding and a mature clematis intertwined with a wisteria, which creep around the façade when in bloom, fool you into believing that the cottage is much older than it really is. Chameleon-like, it blends into the landscape seamlessly. The location is idyllic, looking over a low valley to Roaring Water Bay. With the horizon only eight miles away, it is easy to see the approach of the weather, good or bad, and know you are at its mercy.

Mick and Bernadette have made few structural changes to their home, but with the decorative touches that they have added and all their treasured possessions in place, the cottage, like an old soul, seems to possess a wisdom much greater than its years. The main entrance is through the south-facing, white-plastered sunroom at the back of the cottage. This is a fine place to while away the time, sitting in the white wicker Peacock chair, embracing the view and listening to the deafening silence.

The slate floor in the sunroom continues through to the kitchen. It was the slate kitchen sink and surround with old brass bath taps/faucets that initially sold the cottage to Mick and Bernadette. Although put together by the builder in the 1990s,

ABOVE Ireland's Own *magazine was first published in 1902, costing one penny. More than a hundred years later, the magazine outsells many of its glossy rivals.* **LEFT** *There is no paint chart to label the colour of the kitchen walls, as it was a homemade mix, but it could be described as 'mossy lichen' or, as Bernadette calls it, 'cow dung'!*

the sink looks older, especially with the backdrop of the casement windows and traditional-style window stays. The simple pine table is where these ex-city dwellers spend much of their time on their laptops, developing websites together and keeping in touch with the outside world.

Life is simple here and a far cry from the buzz of the big city. Except for the neighbours' cats and peacocks, and the odd passing donkey, visitors don't just happen by. Unsurprisingly, there is an element of self-sufficiency. Vegetables are grown in the garden, and bread is baked daily in the steam engine of a range; a glossy dark-blue model.

The simply constructed kitchen units were painted by Bernadette, who once made a splendid career out of 'doing' other people's houses. On the shelves, Bernadette keeps a constantly changing display of cherished possessions, arranged by texture and colour. Something of a magpie, she loves to collect all things shiny and gold. Regardless of their monetary value, these items, ranging from a 19th-century hand-painted Satsuma tea set with gold highlights and piles of golden buttons to empty golden syrup tins and a locket of henna-ed hair from her heady youth, are kept behind glass in a cabinet.

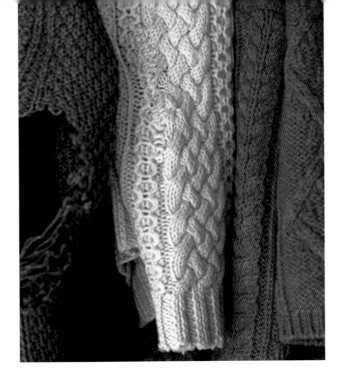

ABOVE *Three much-loved and well-worn Aran jumpers, knitted by Bernadette's mother, are hung patriotically in a colourful formation that resembles the Irish flag. Mrs O'Shea was a versatile woman who, like many young Irish girls, originally trained as a nurse. She also worked as a legal secretary as well as knitting professionally. Such were her skills that she was hired to sit in an Oxford Street shop window demonstrating how to operate a knitting machine!*

Tucked behind the kitchen is the utility area, where the white goods are hidden away behind cream dust-cloth curtains, run up on Bernadette's old Singer sewing machine. This space leads to the only bathroom. Completely wood-panelled, the toilet is a veritable throne, with a mini library on the shelves behind.

A wooden staircase in the centre of the cottage divides the kitchen and living room. The mural on the staircase wall was painted by Bernadette, the in-house artist. It was actually designed to be more a 'cartoon' in the Renaissance sense, made of carved relief plaster, but was never finished. The

novelty of the mural has now worn off and, never one to rest on her laurels, Bernadette is putting her talents to work on something to replace it.

Floor-to-ceiling curtains serve as an optional screen that can separate the kitchen from the living room. Here, an assortment of chairs and a cane sofa, its cushions recently re-covered with red hide, sit in front of a solid-fuel stove. Ireland is not a wooded land (the Vikings and the English took care of that!), but it is rich in peat bogs. For centuries, most households have burned peat, and you can always tell when winter has hit by the sweet and evocative smell hanging in the air. In this home, the ancient tradition continues and peat mixed with a few logs gives the optimum heat.

There is a simple arrangement upstairs under the eaves. One end serves as a work space, with a bed for guests. At the other end is the main bedroom, with a space screened off as a dressing area. Propped up against the wall at the top of the stairs is a large, battered canvas of a gentleman. Bernadette found the painting 30 years ago, abandoned on Islington High Street in London, and dragged it home with her. Close inspection brought to light the spidery signature of John Collier, and research at the National Portrait Gallery in London revealed him to be an eminent Victorian portrait painter. 'Albert', as he is known, has a kindly face, and his benign presence adds to the restful ambience. He seems at home alongside a collection of Aran jumpers, one as tattered as himself. There are piles of shawls and 'hot jars' (hot-water bottles) for the winter nights, but there's no fear of the cold in this home because, as writ large on the blackboard in the kitchen, this is 'Ballydehob... where the sun always shines!'

BELOW *The galley-like bathroom, secreted at the back of the house, resembles the interior of a vintage yacht, with wooden panelling enclosing both the bath and the WC. Facing the window, the cast-iron bath, with its original brass taps/faucets, overlooks the garden and has a view of the bay beyond. Below the window, which is not visible in the picture, is an old butler's sink with the same slate surround as in the kitchen.*

ABOVE *An area under the eaves doubles up as a work space and a guest bedroom. The old, ex-hospital wrought-iron bed has been prettified with a vintage, striped satin, fitted bedspread. The 1920s swivel office chair serves two purposes: as a seat, as originally intended, and also a bedside table. The arched window has a deep ledge, which makes it a lovely place to sit and watch the sunrise.*

With their combined creativity, it was a foregone conclusion that the home of designer Rosalind Walshe and her painter husband Patrick would never be a dull concern.

PARALLEL LIVES

The couple live and work in a pair of cottages, situated in Ballyshemane on the Dublin to Wicklow road. The road didn't even exist when the cottages, originally a farmer's dwelling and a stable, were built in around 1810. Then they were linked to a grand house with its own driveway, but sadly the grand house is no more, and the driveway has returned to fields. Although only 40 minutes' drive from Dublin, their home is in deepest County Wicklow, the Garden of Ireland.

ABOVE *Tiny jars of bold pigment from Morocco make a quirky installation in Rosalind's studio.*
RIGHT *The vibrant kitchen–dining room, with its vivid use of colour, is a warm and inviting space. It is not unheard of for the furniture to be cleared out of the way so that the boys can play rugby! Pots from Africa, inherited English antique furniture, Indian textiles and Irish bowls all combine successfully in the space.*

LEFT *The ornate Indian frame and glass candlestick create the effect of a mini shrine in the vivid blue-painted window recess.*

Patrick was born in Ennis, County Clare, in the 1950s, when horses and carts were still in everyday use. Rosalind hails from Leeds in the north of England. They met in New York in 1982, where Rosalind's career as a young designer was flourishing. Patrick, like many young artists, was forced to supplement his earnings working in restaurant kitchens. The experience paid off – to this day, he rules the roost in the kitchen! They married soon after meeting and moved to LA, but Patrick craved the inspiration of the Irish landscape.

In the early 1990s, Rosalind and Patrick returned slowly to Ireland via India, Indonesia and Africa. In between having her two sons, Rosalind established her

ABOVE LEFT *Traditional Irish cottages were built soundly, their thick walls as much as a metre deep. This solid window ledge makes the perfect setting for an intricate, glass candlestick from The Conran Shop, which, instead of holding candles, provides a nest for ornamental little birds!*
LEFT *The depth of the wood-panelled doorway is even more impressive than the window ledge. A rainbow curtain, reminiscent of Joseph's amazing multicoloured dreamcoat, keeps out any unwanted draughts. A barometer above the door predicts the weather, but you always know when it's summer in Ireland — the rain is warm!*
OPPOSITE FAR RIGHT *Framed drawings of chairs by Armi Maddision, a friend of Rosalind's from art school, hang above one of the Regency dining chairs. The fine chaise longue also dates from the Regency period.*

RIGHT *A butler's tray used as a coffee table proves as convenient as it is portable. Rosalind's favourite mug, given to her by Patrick, is 18th-century spongeware, its design achieved by dabbing on glaze with intricately cut sponges before firing.*

own design business, while Patrick took up his brushes, cocooned in the beauty of the 'wondrous Wicklow mountains'.

The archetypal thick-walled, whitewashed cottage had been inhabited by ten members of the O'Dea clan, all from the same immediate family. Thanks to the low ceilings and partitions, the rooms were tiny and claustrophobic, and there was only one toilet… outside. As a point of reference, electricity only came to Ballyshemane in 1979!

The first job was to get out the sledgehammer and create one large space in the cottage, knocking down walls and the suspended ceiling. The space was then extended to include an up-to-date bathroom – an absolute imperative – and the master bedroom. The end result is a comfortable home completely tailored to the couple's needs.

The front door to the cottage is set slightly off-centre and is still the original size. The interior is a different matter altogether. The removal of the suspended ceiling has created a cathedral-like space and the supporting timber struts make an interesting architectural feature in the living area, which is directly off the kitchen/dining space.

All the walls are painted a uniform off-white and reflect the shocking magenta-pink and cyan-blue on the surrounds of the deep-set windows. A curtain at the front door was the original inspiration for these bold swathes of colour (there's also an acid-green in the hall). Rosalind had the curtain made in Udaipur from a collection of square swatches she had gathered. She asked the tailor to sew them together in a particular order, to create 'a sunset over the lake' effect.

Far from being a showcase, this house is a living, breathing home. The choice of furniture and fittings is a happy assortment – everything

OPPOSITE *Not remotely intimidated by bold colour, Rosalind has used her favourite pink and green for the soft furnishings in the living area. The cushions are made from Designers Guild fabrics and the large chrome lamp came from an operating theatre.*

THIS PAGE *In between exhibitions, Patrick's work is hung all around their home. His inspiration is the landscape around him and he is fascinated by 21st-century-man's relationship with his surroundings.*

looks as if it belongs together naturally. The English Regency sofa from Rosalind's family is a fine antique piece, as are the Regency dining chairs. Upholstered in different-coloured velvets, they are all in good condition and everyday use.

No expense was spared when it came to the comforts of home. A Rangemaster oven has been installed where the old range stood, while a free-standing Godin stove stands in the middle of the living room, providing winter warmth. Comfy armchairs surround it. Covered in sage-green and a favourite magenta fabric, they must have been inspired by that famous curtain, too! At the far

end of the room, French doors lead to the garden. A curtain made up of Kente cloth – a textile woven in narrow strips to tell a story – bought in Ghana has been trimmed with crimson velvet.

The simple bathroom, half of it wood-panelled, is painted in Farrow & Ball's Dead Salmon. Contrasting splashes of colour are provided by the towels. In the bedroom, kilim-covered cushions on the four-poster Balinese wooden bed introduce a touch of vibrancy. Although completely different in style, the traditional English Georgian chest of drawers sits comfortably alongside.

OPPOSITE *The title of 'artist' covers many disciplines. Rosalind attended art school, and although she no longer paints or sculpts, her creativity has found a commercial outlet. A range of china cups she designed, taken from drawings in her architect father's sketchbooks, are instantly recognizable, while her drawing and layout skills can be seen in Avoca's third cookbook. Space, in every sense, is essential for the creative mind and it is here, at her work table, 'playing' with found objects, doodling and looking at art books and magazines, that she formulates her new ideas.*

RIGHT *A mismatched but complementary collection of graphic Moroccan tiles surrounds a window and the sink in Patrick's studio. This craft of* **zellige,** *which has existed in Morocco since the tenth century, uses chips of terracotta tiles covered in enamel, which are then set into plaster.*

As both Rosalind and Patrick work from home, they decided to convert the stable into two separate studios. Patrick's portion, though the smaller of the two, is the more attractive space, with the original stable panelling and tethering posts still intact. A hotchpotch of patterned tiles collected in Morocco forms a decorative splashback around the deep butler's sink. Patrick's output as an artist is prolific, and as well as having numerous shows at home and abroad, in 2006 he was granted a residency at the unique Cill Rialaig Artists' Retreat in County Kerry – a real privilege.

Behind the dividing wall, which sports a large section of carved Balinese panelling, is Rosalind's studio, an Aladdin's cave of old jam jars full of buttons, battered clock cases, rolls of vintage wallpaper and more. Everything and anything she finds that inspires her (a less discerning eye might describe it as junk) will find a place on the weighed-down shelves. Rosalind's design portfolio extends from products to restaurants, books and food, and she also forecasts trends in the world of interiors. At the moment, she is developing a line of quirky handbags transformed from old school satchels and adorned with flotsam, jetsam and a bit of sparkle from her cabinet of curiosities.

Rosalind and Patrick's set-up is a fine example of a combined work and home space, which many strive for but few achieve so successfully. Let's hope that the motto 'A present for my dear girl' – as printed on Rosalind's favourite spongeware mug, a gift from Patrick – is a sign that they will continue to live, work and create together, or side by side at least, happily ever after!

'Ireland, Sir,' said George Bernard Shaw, 'is like no other place under heaven'. Anyone who has visited Ballyvolane House would certainly agree with the sentiment.

GREEN HOUSE

Ballyvolane House, near Castlelyons in north County Cork, is well known for the finest hospitality in the whole of Ireland, and it truly deserves all its many accolades and awards. Its owners, the Green family, are the ultimate hosts.

It was back in the early 1980s that Jeremy and his English wife Merrie first opened their doors to paying guests, being two of the founder members of the Hidden Ireland travel company. However, Ballyvolane is still very much a family home and, at present, four generations live here. A steady stream of friends and family also come to stay, and there is a constant and inescapable air of frivolity.

BELOW *Every evening, dinner is served to all the guests at the formally laid table in the dining room. The chic place settings use modern Willow Pattern plates on top of a larger white charger.*
LEFT *On the long Regency dining table, glass, silverware and china sparkle and shimmer in the candlelight. On the walls, fine ancestral portraits flank the fireplace and a dramatic Chinese ebony, glazed cupboard, brought back from Malaya by Justin's grandparents, contains a magnificent collection of 18th- and 19th-century blue and white ware.*

Ballyvolane is now run by Justin, the oldest of Jeremy and Merrie's three sons, and his Scottish wife Jenny. The couple both worked in the hotel and catering business and they met while working at the Mandarin Oriental Hotel in Hong Kong. Upon returning to the UK, Justin and Jenny managed the hugely successful Babington House in Somerset before bringing their experience and expertise back home to Ireland in 2004. Justin then took on the dubious privilege of running the whole show at Ballyvolane. There can surely be no better man for the task! Justin, quite simply, is a force of nature. Ideas don't stay in his head for very long because he simply and swiftly puts them into practice. The O'Brien Chop House in the heritage town of Lismore, County Waterford, is one good example. Borrowing the idea from London's old chop houses, Justin set up an unpretentious eatery in an old Victorian pub, keeping its original name and serving simple, robust Irish recipes made with local produce. It has been a resounding success.

OPPOSITE BELOW *Homemade marmalade is made in the kitchen, originally the servants' kitchen, to be sold at O'Brien Chop House in Lismore. With Jenny's usual attention to detail, it is stored in a contemporary version of the Kilner jar, which she sourced in Germany. The modern glazed French lantern is made of zinc. Stored safely, high on the top shelf, is a more precious piece — a blue and white tureen that belonged to Justin's grandmother.*

BELOW *The walls in the kitchen are painted in Farrow & Ball's Claydon Blue. By the door is a large framed rural landscape in oil by Justin's grandmother, Wendy Benson, which has hung in this spot forever. Beneath the painting, Mixie the spaniel is ready to run out the door, which leads directly to the farm buildings at the rear. These can be seen through the window above the large old butler's sink, supported on a pair of ceramic columns.*

LEFT *Wriggle is now eight years old. Spaniels, a favourite breed in the Green household, are good pets and, importantly, fine gun dogs. They are thought to originate from Spain, with the name of the breed derived from the country's Latin name,* Hispania.

Back at the ranch, a winding drive, bound on one side by the original iron fencing and on the other by a shrubbery, affords lovely countryside views. The handsome house is a two-storey Italianate version of its former self. Exactly 120 years after it was built in 1728 by the retired Lord Chief Justice of Ireland, Sir Richard Pyne, its owner decided to make major changes, adding a west wing and demolishing the third storey.

The house has ten bedrooms, of which six are for guests. Large and comfortable, they are all individual and traditionally furnished with pieces that have been in the family for generations. Each room is really a suite. One such arrangement, with its hessian-covered walls, looks out over the immaculate terraced gardens and trout lake. A

ABOVE LEFT *Dating from the 1950s, the framed poster advertising grazing land at Ballyvolane was in a neighbour's possession until recently, when Justin brought it back to its rightful home. It now hangs in the hall above various dog leads.*
LEFT *Purely for show is one of a pair of extraordinary antique chairs, fondly referred to as Posh and Becks! Known as fantasy, or grotto, furniture, the chairs are carved, gilded and silvered, with the seat and back taking the form of a large shell.*

large sofa and a Regency drop-leaf pedestal table, with two painted Regency chairs (part of a large set dotted around the rest of the house), make an idyllic little arrangement for lazy breakfasts or for writing (or, more likely nowadays, emailing!). The ensuite bathrooms were installed 20 years ago. Almost as large as the bedrooms, they, too, are classically appointed, some with deep, free-standing cast-iron tubs with ball-and-claw feet and highly polished, chunky brass taps/faucets.

Before dinner, cooked by the in-house chef Teena Mahon and, more often than not, by Jenny as well, guests have the freedom of relaxing in the bright orange, formal pillared entrance hall,

ABOVE *The drawing room walls are wallpapered in a gentle powder blue with a subtle damask-like pattern. Elegant and comfortable seating is provided by an inviting pair of reproduction, deep-buttoned leather chesterfield sofas. The name 'chesterfield' is believed to have originated in the 18th century, when the fourth Earl of Chesterfield, a man of great style and sophistication, commissioned a renowned cabinet-maker to produce a piece of furniture that would 'allow a gentleman to sit upright in utmost comfort'. The large pair of intricately ornate Chinese pots, postioned symmetrically either side of the fireplace, were bought by Justin's father at a local auction. The large glass vase situated on the left of the classical marble mantelpiece is by the Irish-based designer John Rocha, who designs for Waterford Crystal.*

ABOVE *The orange entrance hall boasts fine plaster cornicing and a pair of columns with ornate Corinthian capitals. The room was first painted this shade in 1847, when the house was remodelled, and it has been maintained ever since. The fire remains lit throughout the winter months, offering warmth as soon as you step through the front door. Guests are invited to play the Bluthner baby grand piano.*

LEFT AND FAR LEFT *The winged-back sofa, bought at auction, has a carved wooden frame that would normally be considered ornate but, compared to the base of the coffee table, whose legs are a carved man seemingly bearing the whole weight of the world on his shoulders, it seems relatively plain!*

complete with baby grand piano, which anyone with a modicum of talent is invited to play. Alternatively, there's the option of helping yourself from the 'honesty bar' and sinking into one of the deep-buttoned leather chesterfield sofas by the open fire in the huge drawing room. The piles of books weighing down the coffee table will tell you, in one way or another, all that you'll ever need to know about Ireland.

The large dining room is at the front of the house. Dinner is announced by a large gong, and guests are invited to eat all together at the extending Regency table, which seats at least 12. Flanking the fireplace on both sides is a fine pair of Regency sideboards, which, by day, are protected by old-fashioned place mats. Come the evening, when the room is lit by candles, the rich sheen of the aged wood, created after years of polishing, is revealed. It reflects the sparkle of the candlesticks and the crystal chandelier, creating a

ABOVE LEFT *The complimentary comments in the guest book are heartfelt. The book lives on a desk in a wood–panelled corner under the stairs, just off the entrance hall.*

ABOVE *Leading to the bedrooms is a grand staircase, which benefits from a flood of natural light from the large window on the first return. Lining the walls are paintings inherited through Justin's grandmother and depicting distant ancestors.*

OPPOSITE *Original to the house is this enormous, glazed white terracotta bath, with its highly varnished wood surround — it's so deep that there is a step around the base to help you climb in. Polished to within an inch of their lives, the brass taps/faucets are in direct contrast to the enamelled tin jug; a poor relation but a useful one, for there is no shower in this bathroom. A framed oil painting of the interior of a great church is perfectly placed to highlight the adage 'cleanliness is next to godliness'.*
RIGHT *A pair of headboards painted by Jane Willoughby with dreamlike utopian scenes guarantee a deep and peaceful sleep in this tranquil guest room. The green chair with a fancy valance, to the right of the bed, is a* prie dieu, *or prayer, chair.*

magical scene. Instead of saying grace, Jeremy has been known to relate to diners the story of the night of 4 November 1730, when Andrew St Ledger and his wife, who were renting the house at the time, were murdered in their beds in the room above by a member of the household staff. He tells this tale with a glint in his eye and warns that the room in question is definitely haunted!

The west wing is the working engine of the building. A stainless-steel industrial kitchen was installed in 2005. This is where Teena produces loaves, tarts, cakes and scones every day. Remnants from the original kitchen remain, such as a huge plate rack that's now used to store an array of baking trays, giving a taste of the past.

Alongside the kitchen are several small rooms devoted to storage, including a walk-in larder and a 'Delft' room (traditionally used for storing china), with floor-to-ceiling shelves to support scores of plates, bowls and dishes. In the room that was originally the servants' kitchen, pots of homemade jam and bottles of sloe gin are neatly lined up on the old pine dresser. It's here that the

couple's three children have their supper at the farmhouse table, and also where their cheeky dog sleeps in the armchair. Tidied away in a scruffy Irish press is the assorted apparel of hunting, shooting and fishing – one wonders how there is time to fit in such pursuits!

On a desk in a dark, panelled corner under the main staircase is a large, leather-bound guest book. This is the most recent volume, containing hundreds of signatures from visitors dating back to 1985. It must be so satisfying for the hosts to read over and over again the heartfelt inscriptions for the generous hospitality they have shown.

Rustic
IRISH

Burtown House, a small and perfectly preserved modest mansion just outside the town of Athy in County Kildare, was originally built in 1710 by a Quaker called Robert Power.

STABLE GROUND

Mercifully, Burtown escaped the pillage and arson that destroyed many such houses during the Civil War of 1922–23, and today it is still owned and inhabited by Power's descendents. Over the years, tracts of the estate's 2,000 acres have been sold off, so that what's left today is a relatively modest 200 acres, used as a working farm.

James Fennell, heir to the Burtown estate, has exciting plans for the future, and he and his wife Joanna are nothing but busy. James, one of Ireland's foremost

ABOVE *By retaining the stable doors, the façade hints at the building's original purpose. A formal garden at the front of the house leads to an acre of vegetable garden, which is James's real passion.*
LEFT *The middle door of the stone building leads to the kitchen. Here, Joanna creates delicious vegetarian food with whatever the season yields. The units, made by a local carpenter, are painted a slate-grey/blue hue.*

interior photographers, has 12 books to his name, while Joanna's career as a jewellery designer is on hold as she raises their three young children.

While extensive refurbishment takes place on the house, the Fennells now occupy what was once Burtown's stable block, made up of a pair of stone barns. These have been restored and converted into two separate homes, divided by a formal garden planted with ligustrum topiary lollipops and densely planted lavender – more reminiscent of the South of France than the Irish countryside!

The family has been blessed with more than its fair share of artistic genius. James's grandmother, Wendy Walsh, is one of Ireland's foremost botanical artists, and Lesley Fennell, James's mother, is also an accomplished artist, specializing in portraiture, and with very green fingers, too. The Fennells' aesthetic is informed by this rich heritage and growing up surrounded by fine furniture, art and books. Their own professions and extensive travels have brought an additional dimension to their taste in decoration.

The small entrance hall leads into a cosy living room. Here, a formal bookcase and a Victorian mahogany sideboard are combined with comfy modern sofas and a collection of various birds and animals made in metal by James's cousin in

RIGHT *An antique Regency mahogany desk chair, sometimes referred to as a captain's chair, stands at the head of the kitchen table. It has a deep top rail, and the down-swept supports are typical of the design. Upholstered in black leather, the chair has been in everyday use for nearly 200 years!*

BELOW *A confident mix of styles and periods is seen in the dining room, where a reclaimed railway sleeper/railroad tie acts as the mantelpiece, which is topped with an English Victorian overmantel mirror. A bronze figure of Mercury wings it over trophies from the hunt. On the dining table, a large Kilner jar is used as a vase, in contrast to a grand, albeit rather wonky, candelabra — a family heirloom.*

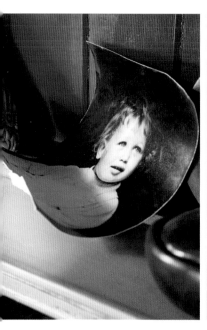

Zimbabwe. Crammed bookshelves flank the fireplace, but there are still more piles of art and photography books stacked on the sideboard. The deep window ledges are home to terracotta pots of pelargoniums brought indoors to escape the harsh winter frosts.

Historically, the dining room was the most important room in the grand old houses of Ireland, as hospitality was paramount, and so it is in James and Joanna's home. The traditional-style Irish dresser has been given a makeover by Joanna, and the scumbled green paint and the raspberry-coloured interior showcase the collection of vessels handsomely. Souvenirs from the hunt and a smattering of fine silver platters and pitchers are mixed with Irish contemporary pottery and a collection of black high-glazed terracotta ware from Sri Lanka.

The dining table was designed by Joanna and constructed by a local carpenter from old railway sleepers/railroad ties, then given a coat of white paint. Very cleverly, a console table was made from the offcuts and serves as an extension to the main table when needed – it's not so very different from the additional leaves that would be added to a fine mahogany dining table when extra guests arrive and need feeding.

In the dining room, no less than five or six different styles of furniture create an eclectic effect. Of particular interest are the two unmatching early 20th-century Irish barber's chairs either side of the Georgian mahogany table below the window. The other seating is a set of early Victorian mahogany balloon-back chairs upholstered in green leather.

ABOVE *At the far end of the house is James's private domain. When he has finished editing photographs after a shoot, he uses this space to make plans for the garden and write songs. In homage to his art, a vintage contraption for viewing slides takes pride of place on the desk. The Perspex coffee was made by an artist friend, Sasha Sykes, as a wedding gift, and encloses* lichen set in resin. It is a beautiful and unique piece.*

OPPOSITE ABOVE *On the hall table sits a framed sheet of stamps designed by Wendy Walsh, James's grandmother. Printed in 1983, they were part of a series of stamps depicting the flora and fauna of Ireland. The Gaelic name for Ireland, Éireann, abbreviated to 'Eire', appears on all Irish stamps.*

Another chunky slab of wood has been installed as a ledge above a contemporary fireplace housing a wood-burning stove. Topping that is an early Victorian gilt overmantel mirror. The effortless blend of materials, styles and periods in this room and throughout this house is proof – if any were needed – that eclecticism is always more interesting than living within the strict confines of any one particular style.

The kitchen, positioned in the middle of the house, has stable doors on both sides, one leading from the formal garden and the other from the farm. It is the hub of the home, and the warming Aga in billiard-table green inspired the choice of

a dark slate-grey/blue colour scheme for the semi-fitted kitchen. The walls are covered with evidence of the family's artistic output – framed still lifes of fruit painted by James's mother hanging alongside family photos taken by James himself.

A ground-floor guest bedroom leads to James's office, a soaring double-height room blessed with maximum daylight, thanks to the lofty floor-to-ceiling French doors. During the winter months in Ireland, the days are short, while at the height of summer it doesn't grow dark until late. This room is more than just an office. James's other passion is music, and it is here, in this inspiring space, that he writes his songs.

BELOW *The living room has a cottagey feel. The full-length windows allow in the maximum amount of light and are draped with sumptuous curtains. This room is a comfortable refuge, perfect for curling up and enjoying one of the many art books on the coffee table and the shelves either side of the open fireplace.*

Upstairs, reached by a staircase from the hall, is another long row of rooms, one leading into the next, which include a child's bedroom, a bathroom, the master bedroom and a dressing room. Carpeted for warmth and quietude, this floor holds yet more fine furniture. The green dressing room has three splendid masculine pieces of Georgian mahogany furniture that provide a contrast to the modern open shelving which covers one wall. In the master bedroom, the sage-green walls showcase an oversized white bed, draped with an ornate, jewel-coloured throw from Jaipur. Wendy Walsh's botanical watercolours are framed and displayed proudly on the walls, and there is a bow-fronted Georgian chest of drawers.

The children's room is home to an Irish, glazed-pine cupboard, packed tightly with teddy bears, and the most splendid rocking horse a child could ever imagine. The horse belonged to James when he was young, and his father before that. Appropriately, the rocking horse joined the family in the old stable, now a beautiful, much-loved home, and allows the children to ride on his back. But it won't be long now before all the restoration work is finished and horse and family can trot back up the drive to the main house whence they came.

ABOVE LEFT *Brogues originate from Scotland and Ireland.*
LEFT *The powder-blue loose cover on this Edwardian armchair is a little threadbare on the arms — not surprising, given that three babies have been nursed in it.*
OPPOSITE ABOVE *The oversized master bed, draped with a decorative throw from Jaipur, is the only modern piece in the sage-green painted bedroom.*
OPPOSITE BELOW *Treasured pieces in the bedroom include photos and paintings, a fragile china doll and an antique rocking horse.*

With a nod to the song, Noelle Campbell-Sharp is a woman you don't meet every day! To name but a few of her many accomplishments, she has, at various times, been a copy writer, publisher, philanthropist and a passionate champion of Ireland's heritage.

A HOUSE FOR ALL SEASONS

Noelle is perhaps, though, proudest of the Cill Rialaig Project, a world-renowned artists' retreat, which she founded in 1993. Similar in some ways to her home, it is made up of ten pre-famine 'cabins', converted into individual dwellings/studios for carefully selected invitees, coming 'from Beijing to Buenos Aires'. An advocate of the arts, Noelle is passionate about giving artists the freedom to express themselves, and 2,500 free places at the retreat have been granted to artists since the project's foundation.

Brought up in County Wexford by adoptive parents in the 1950s, Noelle was educated at the local convent but left before she was 16, having decided that the nuns had taught her too much already! She entered the world of publishing, eventually becoming Ireland's answer to American *Vogue*'s Anna Wintour, but with her individualistic attire and her mop of now-orange curls, she is more often mistaken for Vivienne Westwood! In the mid-1980s, Noelle fell in love with the wild

ABOVE RIGHT *Against the outside wall of the bar leans an enormous anchor; the bar's namesake.*

OPPOSITE *The iconic advertising posters for Guinness were first drawn in the 1930s by the English artist John Gilroy. Various instruments sit waiting in the bar for the next music session. The circular case contains an Irish drum, called a Bodhrán.*

RIGHT *The stout drunk in these parts is Murphy's, brewed in nearby Cork city. A drop of Irish whiskey as a chaser makes a fine combination!*

FAR RIGHT *The black panelling and red ceiling in The Anchor Bar put one in the right frame of mind for drinking.*

and rugged landscape of South Kerry, specifically Ballinskelligs, on the tip of the Iveragh Peninsula. With her extensive knowledge of Irish history and the vernacular stone buildings of the region, which were mostly in ruins, she was undaunted by the idea of taking on the restoration of a 1790s extended stone farm building, known as a *clóchan*. Together with celebrated Irish architect Alfred Cochrane and several stone masons (one of whose ancestors had worked on the original construction), work was completed in 1989.

On the side of a scraggy hillside, facing the sea and nine miles from the nearest town, the house, made up of four connected buildings, with a self-contained guest apartment in the square tower, is like a chameleon, almost invisible from the road, as its colours merge into the hills behind. This is now Noelle's second home – she mainly lives in Dublin – but she visits at least once a month and stays for the whole of the long summer. Though all the buildings here are built from stone, they are far from cold because they are blessed with natural

light from dawn till dusk. Nevertheless, the storage heaters are always on during winter, and the turf fire smoulders silently come evening time.

These buildings would originally have been home to various family strands of peasant farmers, with as many as 15 people living in each one. It is impossible to appreciate how harsh life would have been back then. With no running water and no electricity, and being at the mercy of the ever-changing elements, where the wind often reaches hurricane speeds, lord knows how they kept warm! Potatoes were the main crop, and the land had to be tilled by hand – horses were only for the wealthy. There is still evidence in the fields around nearby Bolus Head of hand-tilled ridges. It is a humbling place to be, although the sheer unspoilt beauty of the area, empowering and uplifting, detracts from the weight of the knowledge of what happened to these people during the Great Potato Famine of the mid-19th century.

OPPOSITE *The views from inside the Sky Room are spectacular. The glass roof is like a permanently changing painting above you. As the saying goes, 'If you don't like the weather, stick around for five minutes.' A visiting Italian artist was most dismayed when he woke to Mediterranean–blue skies several mornings in a row, having made the trip for dramatic weather and inspiration!*

ABOVE LEFT *Across the country there are still vast tracts of peat bogs, and a state-owned company,* Bord na Móna, *is responsible for managing peat production. In its processed form, peat is densely compressed into oblong bars and sold in bales of 20–24 'briquettes'. In more rural areas, turf, which is dried-out sods of peat, is more commonly used. The turf in the two large baskets, which comes from the bog on Noelle's land, has dried grass on it, indicating that the bog is little used.*

ABOVE RIGHT *There are ten acres of land around the house, and when standing in the garden, with your back to the sea, you can see that the façade of the house is completely in keeping with the surrounding landscape. Any Kerry man will tell you there are only two kingdoms: the kingdom of God and the kingdom of Kerry. One is not of this world and the other is out of this world!*

ABOVE *Washing was traditionally done on Mondays and ironing on Tuesdays, using flat irons such as the first two displayed here.* **LEFT** *When migrants set sail from Ireland during the Potato Famine, they often took with them a stool like this one, as there was no seating on the coffin ships. It's in use here as a side table.* **OPPOSITE** *The chair, in all its forms, is probably the oldest of all types of furniture found in Ireland. Items like this 19th-century settle table, which converts from a seat to a table, were made to fit a specific space and be multifunctional. The sculpture on the ledge above the fireplace is by Orla de Bri.*

One of the first restoration jobs was to rebuild all the crumbling stone walls, connect the four buildings and put in the six front doors! The entrance used most frequently now is the double glazed doors of the Sky Room. So-called for obvious reasons, the Sky Room has a steeply-pitched roof of glass. It was originally the cow house, but now serves as the entrance hall.

During reconstruction, a huge, stone heraldic plaque was embedded into the structure of the chimney wall in the Sky Room. Noelle bought this 17th-century piece in a Dublin antiques shop, but

it has no place here historically, as it was probably from Ulster originally – the three hands are the emblem of the province. Nevertheless, it is now the main feature of this room and makes an impressive statement at that.

The furniture in the Sky Room is a melange of vernacular Irish seating around a draped, glass-topped iron table. Decorating the room are various mementoes that visiting guests have left behind as a thank you, including sculptures and paintings, as well as an installation put together by the Irish artist Mick Mulcahy and Donovan,

the 1960s Scottish singer, which comprises a broomstick, a vintage dress and some wind chimes!

If the former inhabitants of this *clóchan* were to suddenly come back to earth, they would have a great time of it, for this must surely be the only private house in Ireland with its very own pub! What's more, it's the very best pub in the land for one simple reason – it's unlicensed, and so the drinks are free. Christened The Anchor Bar, this dark and snug space, complete with a cosy corner that lends itself to impromptu musical sessions, is to the right of the Sky Room. Murphy's stout is available on tap, but if that's not your poison, anything else you choose to ask for can be found on the shelves. Black-painted captain's chairs, dark panelling and waxed cloth-covered card tables are as authentic as you can get, and there is also a pair of *prie dieu* chairs (prayer chairs) in case someone suddenly feels the need!

OPPOSITE *A pair of blue-painted chairs with yellow straw seats are a modern take on the traditional* súgán *design. The bookcase incorporates a ladder to a secret space, sometimes used as an extra bedroom and particularly loved by younger visitors.*

ABOVE *The display of paintings is constantly changing but, for the moment, these are the favoured three in the living room.*

Above the pub is the master bedroom, a sparse but comfortable room with a big traditional brass bed. At first glance, the walls look as if they are simply painted white, but on close inspection you can see an intricate Celtic pattern etched into the wet plaster. Created by a local circus artist, John Schultz, the pattern gives the room a subtle depth that is complemented by the soft cotton drapes at the windows and the textured Masala bedspread.

At the opposite end of the house, the east wing comprises a darker, more traditional room. The turf fire here is in a grate, a forerunner to the

ABOVE LEFT *'Lay, lady, lay/Lay across my big brass bed. Whatever colours you have in your mind…' In answer to Bob Dylan, only white, sir. Purity, cleanliness and innocence! The mistress's chamber is light-filled and sparse.*

ABOVE CENTRE *The beautiful Irish lace curtain hanging at the window was handmade by Gretta Janssen.*

range, being half oven and half open fire. Only the chimney wall is bare stone; the others are wallpapered in a soft yellow stripe, giving a warmer feel. A 19th-century settle table, a vernacular piece most commonly found in the south-east of Ireland, performs exactly as its name suggests, converting from a large seat into a table for everyday use. It provides the main seating in this room and is softened with Irish spun blankets from Cleo. Additional seating is offered by two hedge chairs – the name stems from the different woods found in hedgerows that the chairs were originally made from – with snug felted cushions made by the Dingle artist Una Ní Shé.

It is in this room (and the bar) that the conversations continue into the early hours, whether they be discussing complicated Irish politics, imagining a conversation between James Joyce and W. B. Yeats or recalling the visit of the Irish playwright John Millington Synge to the *seanchai* (storyteller) Sean O'Connaill's house in

TOP RIGHT *The water glass is one of a number that Noelle bought directly from the artist. Each piece is hand-blown and unique.*

LEFT *An unframed landscape on the mantelpiece is reminiscent of the cabins at the artists' retreat Cill Rialaig, which Noelle founded on Bolus Head, a mile down the road.*

nearby Cill Rialaig village. There is another guest bedroom beyond this room, with two single brass beds covered in neutral wool blankets from Paul Costelloe's home collection. The walls look as if they have been decorated with striped wallpaper in a faded mushroomy pink, but they are, in fact, hand-painted – and all the more attractive for it, with their wonky lines!

Passionate about both her Irish heritage and Irish culture, Noelle is most definitely a force to be reckoned with. Her home, 'Ceannuig', is a true reflection of this passion and, just like the Cill Rialaig Project, it is a place the likes of which you will not come across every day.

ABOVE *Found in a state of disrepair, the vintage twin beds with brass finials in the downstairs guest bedroom were renovated and painted. Beds like these were first made in the 1850s up until the First World War. Of course, modern reproduction brass beds are now available, but they don't make 'em like they used to!*

RIGHT *The stoneware 'adaptable hot water bottle and bed warmer' hanging from the end of the bed was sold by Boots the Chemist in 1908.*

SOURCE DIRECTORY

ANTIQUES

A&L ANTIQUES
284 Lillie Road
London SW6 7PX
+44 20 7610 2694
www.aandlantiques.co.uk
Farmhouse tables, cupboards, chests and upholstery.

ANN-MORRIS ANTIQUES
239 East Sixtieth Street
New York, NY 10022
+1 212 755 3308
Reproduction lamps and shades.

DENZIL GRANT
www.denzilgrant.com
Antique folk art and fine provincial furniture.

GEOFFREY BREEZE
www.antiquecanes.co.uk
Antique canes and walking sticks.

GORRY GALLERY
www.gorrygallery.ie
Gallery specializing in Irish art from the 17th–21st century.

JOSEPHINE RYAN ANTIQUES
www.josephineryan antiques.co.uk
Chandeliers, antique mirrors, furniture and accessories.

O'SULLIVAN ANTIQUES
www.osullivanantiques.com
Fine Irish antiques in both Dublin and New York.

ROBERT YOUNG
68 Battersea Bridge Road
London SW11 3AG
+44 20 7228 7847
www.robertyoungantiques.com
Antique country furniture.

TARA
6 Church Street
London NW8 8ED
+44 20 7724 2405
Decorative antiques

TIM BOWEN
Ivy House
Ferryside
Carmarthenshire
SA17 5SS
+44 1267 267122
www.timbowenantiques.co.uk
Welsh vernacular furniture.

WELDON'S
55 Clarendon Street
Dublin 2
Ireland
+353 1 677 1638
www.weldons.ie
Antique Irish silver.

ARCHITECTURAL FEATURES

ARCHITECTURAL PANELING
www.apaneling.com
Reproduction fireplaces, paneling and moldings.

CARAVATI'S INC.
104 East Second Street
Richmond, VA 23224
+1 804 232 4175
www.caravatis.com
Architectural salvage.

CHESNEYS
194–200 Battersea Park Road
London SW11 4ND
+44 20 7627 1410
www.chesneys.co.uk
Antique and reproduction fireplaces and stoves.

KILKENNY ARCHITECTURAL SALVAGE AND ANTIQUES
The Old Woollen Mills
Bleach Road
Kilkenny
Ireland
+353 56 7764434
www.eurosalve.com
Antique and salvaged materials.

LASSCO
www.lassco.co.uk
Architectural salvage and reclaimed materials.

WALCOT RECLAMATION
www.walcot.com
Reclaimed architectural features and building materials.

ART

JULIAN CHICHESTER.
www.julianchichester.co.uk
Silk-screen prints such as the one shown on page 91.

GREENLANE GALLERY
Holy Ground
Dingle
County Kerry
Ireland
+353 66 915 2018
www.greenlanegallery.com
Contemporary paintings and sculpture by leading Irish artists.

ORIEL GALLERY
Clare Street
Dublin 2
Ireland
+353 1 676 3410
www.theoriel.com
Quality Irish paintings.

THE ORIGIN GALLERY
83 Harcourt Street
Dublin 2
Ireland
+353 1 4785259
origingallery@hotmail.com
Fine Irish paintings, sculptures and ceramics.

THE BARBARA STANLEY GALLERY
279 Upper Richmond Road
London SW15 6SP
+44 20 8789 8088
www.irishartinlondon.com
Contemporary Irish art.

CRAFTS AND CERAMICS

JOE HOGAN BASKETS
Loch na Fooey
Finny, Clonbur
County Galway
Ireland
+353 94 954 8241
www.joehoganbaskets.com
Irish baskets similar to the one shown on page 32.

NICHOLAS MOSSE POTTERY
Bennettsbridge
County Kilkenny
Ireland
+353 56 772 7505
www.nicholasmosse.com
Pottery in the style of traditional 18th-century Irish Spongeware.

ROSEMARIE DURR POTTERY
Castlecomer Estate Yard
Castlecomer
County Kilkenny
Ireland
+353 56 444 0007
www.rosedurr.com
Hand-thrown pottery.

STEPHEN PEARCE POTTERY
The Old Pottery
Shanagarry
County Cork
Ireland
+353 21 464 6807
Handmade organic pottery.

KITCHENS

AGA OVENS
www.aga-ranges.com (US)
www.aga-web.co.uk (UK)
Manufacturers of the iconic AGA range cooker.

FROYLE TILES LTD
The Hambledon Pottery
Hambledon Road
Hambledon
Surrey GU8 4DR
+44 1428 684111
www.froyletiles.co.uk
Hand-made glazed tiles.

PLAIN ENGLISH
www.plainenglishdesign.co.uk
Beautifully simple kitchens.

LIGHTING

HECTOR FINCH LIGHTING
www.hectorfinch.com
Simple and beautiful lighting.

VAUGHAN
www.vaughandesigns.com
Stylish and classical lighting, including lanterns such as the one on page 88.

PAINT

FARROW & BALL
www.farrow-ball.com
Paint in subtle, muted shades.

OLD FASHIONED MILK PAINT COMPANY
www.milkpaint.com
Paints from natural pigments.

TABLEWARE

JOHN LEWIS
www.johnlewis.com
Stockists of John Rocha's range for Waterford Crystal as well as Wedgwood's white fine bone china, as seen on page 48.

WILLIAM YEOWARD
www.williamyeowardcrystal.com
Modern crystal, silver and china inspired by antique crystal pieces and all made by hand.

TEXTILES

AVOCA
www.avoca.ie
From its humble beginnings as a modest weaving mill, the Avoca empire now spans womenswear, soft furnishings, food halls, cafes, cookbooks and a garden plus nursery. Visit their website for details of their stores and to shop online.

BLARNEY WOOLLEN MILLS
Blarney
County Cork
Ireland
+353 21 451 6111
www.blarney.com
Fine wools and tweeds as well as other quality Irish goods.

GIVAN'S IRISH LINEN
+44 1733 562 300
www.givans.co.uk
Pure Irish linen for the home and by the metre.

KATHERINE M IRELAND TEXTILES AND DESIGN
65–69 Lots Road
London SW10 0RN
+44 20 7751 4554
and at
636 N. Almont Drive
Los Angeles
CA 90069
+1 310 246 1906
www.kathrynireland.com
Relaxed, colourful fabrics and wallpapers plus bedding, pillows and lampshades.

LISBETH MULCAHY
Siopa na bhFíodóirí,
Sráid an Dóirín,
Daingean Uí Chúis
(Dingle)
County Kerry
Ireland
+353 66 915 16 88
www.lisbethmulcahy.com
Tapestries and woven goods from one of Ireland's best known weavers and tapestry artists.

LUNN ANTIQUES
86 New Kings Road
London SW6 4LU
+44 20 7736 4638
www.lunnantiques.co.uk
Antique and modern linen.

BUSINESS CREDITS

Architects, designers and business owners whose work is featured in this book:

BALLYVOLANE HOUSE &
BLACKWATER SALMON FISHERY
Castlelyons
County Cork
Ireland
T: +353 25 36349
E: info@ballyvolanehouse.ie
www.ballyvolanehouse.ie
Pages 8 below left and centre; 122 –131; 160.

SUSAN CALLERY
www.greenlanegallery.com
www.dinglehorseriding.com
Pages 9 above left and above right; 10–11; 24–31.

NOELLE CAMPBELL-SHARP
FORMER PUBLISHER, NOW
DIRECTOR OF ORIGIN GALLERY
83 Harcourt Street
Dublin 2
Ireland
T: +35 3 1 4785259
E: theorigingallery@gmail.com
Pages 5 above left; 7 above left; 7 centre; 132–133; 144–153.
and
ARCHITECT: ALFRED COCHRANE
Corke Lodge
Woodbrook
Bray
County Wicklow
Ireland
M: +353 872 447 006
E: Alfred@corkelodge.com

www.alfredcochrane.com
Pages 5 above left; 7 above left; 7 centre; 132–133; 144–153.

PHILIPPA DEVAS
DEVAS DESIGNS
22 Halsey Street,
London SW3 2QH
Tel: 020 7584
E: mail@devasdesigns.co.uk
www.devasdesigns.co.uk
Pages 5 below left; 9 below left; 44–53.

KIM DREYER
ARCHITECT M.R.I.A.I.
DREYER ASSOCIATES
ARCHITECTURAL·URBAN·DESIGN
T: +353 404 42818
E: kd@dreyerassociates.com
www.dreyerassociates.com
Pages 7 below centre; 8 above right; 12–23.

JAMES FENNELL
www.jamesfennell.com
Pages 134–143.

TRICIA FOLEY
E: tricia@triciafoley.com
www.triciafoley.com
Pages 5 below left; 9 below left; 44–53.

BERNADETTE O'SHEA
www.diaspora.ie
www.ballydehob-t-shirts.com
Pages 7 below left; 8 below right; 104–113.

AMANDA PRATT
CREATIVE DIRECTOR
AVOCA
www.avoca.ie
Pages 8 above left; 9 below centre; 42–43; 54–67.

MARY JANE RUSSELL
TOWN AND COUNTRY
T: +353 872 364939
E: info@tandc.ie
www.tandc.ie
Pages 82–101.

ROSALIND AND PATRICK WALSHE
www.patrick-walshe.com
Pages 7 above centre; 7 centre right; 114–121.

TAD WILBUR'S MUSIC IS AVAILABLE
TO LISTEN TO AT:
www.myspace.com/tadwilbur
Pages 1–4; 5 above right; 7 above right; 9 below right; 92–103

PICTURE CREDITS

All photography by James Fennell.

Front endpapers The home of Dr Noelle
Campbell-Sharp, founder of Cill Rialaig Project
(architect: Alfred Cochrane); 1–4 The home of
Tad Wilbur in Co. Sligo; 5 above left The home of
Dr Noelle Campbell-Sharp, founder of Cill Rialaig
Project (architect: Alfred Cochrane); 5 above right
The home of Tad Wilbur in Co. Sligo; 7 above left
The home of Dr Noelle Campbell-Sharp, founder
of Cill Rialaig Project (architect: Alfred Cochrane);
7 above centre The home of the designer Rosalind
Walshe and painter Patrick Walshe in Co. Wicklow;
7 above right The home of Tad Wilbur in Co.
Sligo; 7 centre the home of Dr Noelle Campbell-
Sharp, founder of Cill Rialaig Project (architect:
Alfred Cochrane); 7 centre right The home of the
designer Rosalind Walshe and painter Patrick
Walshe in Co. Wicklow; 7 below left The home of
Bernadette O'Shea in Co. Cork; 7 below centre
The family home of the architect Kim Dreyer in
Co. Wicklow; 8 above left The home of Amanda
Pratt, Creative Director, Avoca; 8 above right The
family home of the architect Kim Dreyer in Co.
Wicklow; 8 below left and centre the home of
Justin & Jenny Green, owners of Ballyvolane
House; 8 below right The home of Bernadette
O'Shea in Co. Cork; 9 above left and above right
The home of Susan Callery, owner of Greenlane
Gallery in Dingle www.greenlanegallery.com;
9 below centre the home of Amanda Pratt,
Creative Director, Avoca; 9 below right The home
of Tad Wilbur in Co. Sligo; 10–11 The home of
Susan Callery, owner of Greenlane Gallery, in
Dingle www.greenlanegallery.com; 12 –23
The family home of the architect Kim
Dreyer in Co. Wicklow; 24–31 The home of
Susan Callery, owner of Greenlane Gallery,
in Dingle www.greenlanegallery.com; 42 –43

Amanda Pratt, Creative Director, Avoca;
54– 67 Amanda Pratt, Creative Director, Avoca;
82–101 The family home of the interior decorator
Mary Jane Russell of 'Town & Country', Cork;
92 –103 The home of Tad Wilbur in Co. Sligo;
104–113 The home of Bernadette O'Shea in Co.
Cork; 114–121 The home of the designer Rosalind
Walshe and painter Patrick Walshe in Co. Wicklow;
122–131 the home of Justin & Jenny Green, owners
of Ballyvolane House; 132–133 the home of
Dr Noelle Campbell-Sharp, founder of Cill
Rialaig Project (architect: Alfred Cochrane);
134–143 The family home of photographer
James Fennell in Co. Kildare; 144–153 the home
of Dr Noelle Campbell-Sharp, founder of Cill
Rialaig Project (architect: Alfred Cochrane);
157 The home of Tad Wilbur in Co. Sligo; 159
& 160 the home of Justin & Jenny Green, owners
of Ballyvolane House.

INDEX

ACKNOWLEDGMENTS

The making of this book has given me the privilege of spending a day in 13 beautiful Irish homes, all of them very different but each one reflecting the personalities of their idiosyncratic and creative owners. It is they who merit my first thanks for extending genuine hospitality and enthusiasm, and allowing me to photograph their homes. I feel as if I have made a whole new group of friends.

In particular, thanks go to Bernadette O'Shea, a kindred spirit and a daughter of the Irish Diaspora, whose interest and help on this project was totally unselfish. Thanks, too, to Noelle Campbell-Sharp, creator of the Cill Rialaig Project, for allowing me to stay as a guest in what is the most beautiful and inspiring place on earth.

Thanks to James Fennell for making the day's work such fun and taking more shots than we could ever hope to publish. As always, many thanks to the team at RPS for allowing me to make this book happen, and to Helen Ridge for her faithful edit.

My beautiful children Cathal and Uma Rose are growing up so fast. I miss them desperately when they are with their father, but know they are safe in his loving care. I hope that with their quarter Irish blood, they will always love Ireland as I do.

The circle of life is strange. In 1986, I spent a blissful time in a thatched cottage by the River Slaney in Tomhaggard, County Wexford. There was a boy involved, of course! But true love never runs smooth, and I returned to London and got over my broken heart. Unexpectedly, 23 years later, the boy from that cottage came back into my life. And it is with him, Howard Peter Fairbrass, that I now share my life and my logs! Thank you, God!